Table of Contents

Narcissistic Abuse Recovery

Everything the victims need to know to healing after hidden abuse and breaking down narcissism, empaths and codependency

Dr. Theresa J. Covert

Introduction

Y ou may have heard that you can't find love until you learn to love yourself. This is often true of most things. You can't learn to be patient with others until you learn to be patient with yourself.

There is a multitude of activities you can do to improve upon your patience with yourself. It is crucial for your ability to recover and develop new relationships. You must learn to guard yourself against entering into another relationship with a narcissist but it is also important that you do not become so impatient with anything that reminds you of the narcissist in your past that you struggle to form new relationships.

The world is a more stimulating place than the narcissist you were with made it feel. You will need to come up with new activities to find yourself in the world again. The relationship you were in with a narcissist attacked your sense of identity, boundaries, reality, and control. You will need to actively participate in activities that put you back to a place where you can reclaim your sense of identity and control.

Your goal is to find activities to reestablish what was taken from you. You will want to find a relationship in which reciprocation is readily available and understood as important. You have the tools in your home, neighborhood, and backyard to rebuild your boundaries and reclaim your identity.

Actively pursue your sense of self. Recognize how it was stifled and how you can get it back. Admitting that there has been a problem in your life that caused you to lose your sense of identity will be crucial for your recovery. You must get out into the world and find your place again. You must reclaim it without the narcissist you were in a relationship with previously.

When you were with a narcissist, both of you gazed into them. Now it is time for you to start practicing gazing inward toward yourself and then outward toward other things than the narcissist that convinced you that your gaze was most worthwhile when it was on them.

This is how we move between turning inward and turning outward. What you will be learning to do once again is honor your self-awareness and your ability to turn inward and outward. The reason for this is that you have had your gaze turned toward the narcissist for a long time. It is time to turn it toward yourself and others.

It is vital to your recovery that you neither get stuck retreating back into yourself nor outward without reclaiming your sense of identity. The narcissist you were with was empty inside. He or she tried to empty you too. Don't be like them. You must find the substance within yourself without forgetting to do what the narcissist struggled to do—look outside of yourself too. You need to make these passages. You need to find yourself without getting stuck there. Only once you accept the abuse you experienced can you move past it. It is time for you to acknowledge it and face reality in the way the narcissist could not.

Chapter1:
Narcissist

S ome people might view a highly confident person as somewhat narcissistic. The easiest way to distinguish between the two is to look at their behavior and personality. A narcissist is unable to be humble, but someone who is simply highly confident can exhibit strong self-esteem, but still be humble. When someone is considered to have healthy narcissism, it means that they can get through difficult times by experiencing joy in themselves. This is associated with self-worth and self-esteem. What's important is to find a balance between narcissism and empathy, which lie at opposite ends of a scale.

We all need some empathy to function within society, but we also need to be somewhat selfish and detached from our empathetic perceptions from time to time. As a culture, we tend to deify the idea of a completely selfless individual, but in real-world experience, entirely selfless people can be grating, miserable, and difficult to deal with. They also teach others to view and treat them as inferior when they consistently put their own needs last. They empathize with everyone and thus can become drowned in emotional experiences.

The idea of a completely self-centered individual to the point of envisioning them as a demon or monster, with no soul and no emotional substance. Though, a narcissist can be awfully charming and fun to be around—for short periods, at least. They train others to see them as superior by consistently putting their own needs first. And while their thought patterns are distorted in such a way as to stifle empathetic practice, narcissists experience the same range of emotions as most other people. Their emotions simply prompt them to behave differently. Under the surface, they are no different than anyone else.

The narcissist feels entitled to put their own needs ahead of everyone else's, even when the circumstances should prompt them to do just the opposite. They also have trouble putting themselves in the shoes of those around them, so they struggle to comprehend why their requests might be unreasonable, or why their expectations might be difficult for others to meet.

Types of Narcissist

There are many kinds of narcissists out there, while reading these descriptions, stay mindful of the fact that these types are not fixed; a narcissist can evolve from one type into another, or even embody a unique blend of two or more types.

The Grandiose Narcissist

The grandiose or classic narcissist is the kind of person that we typically think of when we imagine a narcissist cliché. They are extremely vain, condescending and arrogant, bold and charismatic, bombastic, and unashamed of their quest to acquire limitless power and prestige.

They are often so audacious in their narcissistic statements and behaviors that some will presume they are being sarcastic or comedic when they are in fact being quite genuine. People may laugh it off when this person mocks those that they consider beneath them, or launches into a monologue of self-praise, thinking that this is a show put on for the sake of entertaining others, ironically failing to see that this is the narcissist's honest expression of personal opinion. Unfortunately, laughter or silent acceptance reactions can reinforce the narcissist's inflated sense of self-importance, as they interpret these as signs of agreement or approval.

Grandiose narcissists also tend to have a childlike lack of self-awareness, choosing behaviors that virtually scream, "Look at me! Look at me!" They are usually comfortable speaking highly of themselves while belittling others with such brazen confidence that one might wonder if they have never been taught that such behavior is considered rude.

This narcissistic type is likely to have the least shame in expressing their egocentric attitudes; this may be due to their genuine belief that they are obviously and strikingly better than everyone around them, and the accompanying assumption that this flamboyant peacocking is what others expect of them. For example, if a member of a foreign country's royal family met you but refused to shake your hand or make eye contact, you might accept their display of arrogance, considering their title. A grandiose narcissist might struggle to understand why you wouldn't extend the same courtesy and respect to them. Though you may see yourself as more or less their equal, they believe themselves to be superior to you and everyone else, so their haughtiness and vanity are justified in their minds.

The Closet Narcissist

The closet narcissist is also called a "covert" narcissist. They have the same competitive, defensive, and shame avoidant mindset as any other narcissist type, but they express it stealthily, flying under the radar. While a grandiose narcissist can be loud and showy, using bravado to mask their insecurities, the closet narcissist's preferred tactic is silence. This isn't a submissive or reticent silence; it is pointed and deliberate. While keeping their lips sealed, they can assert their status and superiority by judging others and ever refusing to make themselves vulnerable to similar judgment.

The closet narcissist feels conflicted about their thirst for attention. The closet narcissist might define their self-worth and feel special based on their proximity to something unique, desirable, and unattainable—or their relationship with a person who embodies the same qualities. For example, a closet narcissist may not be particularly boastful or ostentatious about it but choose to dress in elite designer brands from head to toe, hoping that only other special people of a similar degree of importance might recognize them as a member of the same club. Or, they might find their source of superiority by befriending celebrities or powerful politicians. Covert narcissists tend to make excellent assistants to high-powered bosses, talent managers, and behind-the-scenes orchestrators; just beyond the reach of the spotlight, they can stand beside the star and pull all the strings from a comfortable, well-shielded position.

They struggle to maintain personal relationships or start them since they aren't as confident, charismatic, or overtly charming as their grandiose counterparts. When they do build any type of close relationship, though, they often develop a two-faced demeanor, presenting one personality to the outside world and exhibiting just the opposite when alone with a "loved" one.

They commonly use snobbery to belittle others, looking down their noses at them rather than explicitly insulting them with words.

For example, a closet narcissist could become obsessed with exercise, perfecting their body shape through hours and hours of work at the gym each week—but when offered a compliment on their sculpted figure, they would not want to admit that it took effort on their part, preferring instead to pretend that the shape is natural and easy for them to carry. Or, they might admit to the hard work but claim they were motivated by health or happiness, rather than a desperate need to be admired.

A closet narcissist is a master of disguise, using feigned humility, shyness, or a charitable demeanor to mask the self-centered motivations behind all their actions. They may not be likely to brag about their achievements, financial successes, or romantic conquests, and they might not draw attention to themselves through physical grooming or dynamic, showy behaviors; instead, this type is more likely to seek attention from others in the form of sympathy or pity.

The Malignant Narcissist

Malignant or toxic narcissists are rarer than both the grandiose and covert types, which is lucky for the rest of us. If you've ever known a true malignant narcissist, you understand what a volatile and destructive force this personality disorder can be. People who earn this title typically suffer from a combination of narcissistic personality disorder along with one or more others, such as antisocial personality disorder, manic or compulsive behavioral issues, paranoia, or sadistic inclinations. They are often the easiest narcissists to recognize, as they are usually unable to achieve the same degrees of success that grandiose or covert narcissists can grasp.

Without real evidence of their superiority, in the form of money, status, power, educational degrees, or social support, it can be overwhelmingly obvious to others that the malignant narcissist has an unrealistic opinion of their own importance. It is not obvious to the malignant narcissist, though.

Malignant narcissists tend to see the world through a lens of dichotomies, the most important of which is "me versus everyone and everything else." They have trouble understanding grey areas or multifaceted concepts, preferring to define everything as either good or bad, right or wrong, love or hate, yes or no, now or never. They also have an impulse to turn everything into a competition, applying the logic of scarcity to circumstances where it isn't necessary; for example, at a pizza party with more food and more seating than is needed to accommodate everyone's needs, the malignant narcissist might get bent out of shape over who takes the largest slice of any particular pie, or who claims the seat that they consider most optimal, even though there's more than enough to go around.

The malignant narcissist is the most dangerous of the three types. At times, their behavior can be indistinguishable from that of the criminally psychopathic. They see no problem with causing pain for others to an end; in some cases, they may even derive pleasure from causing emotional or physical harm to their victims, enjoying the rush of sadistic power it provides for them.

Chapter2:
Sub-Types of Narcissists

Overt and Covert

D escribed as in using methods to get their needs met are more upfront and public or more secretive and stealth.

Sub-types have characteristics that are related to the type of narcissist that they are. An example of this is an Overt and Covert Sub-Types. These sub-types may both insult a person they perceive to be a threat because they have a better pedigree than the narcissist. As we know, narcissists have a self-image that is far better than anyone else all the while protecting their fragile ego and insecurities.

Both Overt and Covert Sub-Types will put this person down, be boastful, and seek opportunities to use people to fulfill their needs. However, the Overt Narcissists will do so in a noticeable, public way, whereas the Covert Narcissists will be quieter and more passive-aggressive about it.

Overt Narcissists will be more out in the open about using manipulative methods to have their needs fulfilled. Covert narcissists will use more underhanded ways to be manipulative where a person on the receiving end of being manipulated is not quite sure if they were manipulated or not.

A possible example of an Overt Narcissist is a Bully Narcissist. This is a narcissist who builds themselves up by embarrassing and humiliating other people. They share traits in common with the Grandiose Narcissist, but they are cruel in the way they declare their superiority.

They frequently depend on disrespect and disdain in order to make others feel as if they are losers, elevating their ego and proving themselves to be a winner.

They will mock and belittle the other person and when they want something from the other person, they may become threatening if their need isn't fulfilled.

Along the line of Covert Narcissists, the Seductive Narcissist can fall into this category. This type of narcissist covertly manipulates the other person by making them feel good about themselves. To get the other person to do their bidding, they complement and admire them so that, over time, the other person begins to like and admire the narcissist.

Somatic and Cerebral

Sub-Type 2 is described by what primarily the narcissist values in themselves and others.

Neither of these sub-types wishes that their partner outshines them, but they want to have someone around who boosts their status. To the narcissist, their partners are to be shown off to others as if they were objects added to a collection.

Somatic narcissists are absorbed with their external appearance, how youthful they look, the clothing they buy and wear, and how well their bodies look in those clothes. They can't pass a mirror without checking out their reflection and spend an inordinate amount of time at the gym.

Cerebral narcissists think they know it all and that they have stellar intelligence. They're always ready to give their opinion even when no one asks them for it. They know more than anyone in the room about any topic, no matter what the conversation is about.

They try impressing others with their positions of power and achievements.

Inverted

Researchers have found that researchers have a specific type of vulnerable, covert narcissist known as an Inverted Narcissist.

This is a codependent sub-type. They feel that in order to feel special they need to attach themselves to other narcissists. They are only happy when they have relationships with other narcissists. They suffered from abandonment issues as a child and are also called victim-narcissists.

Narcissist, the term so often used in arbitrary ways, has made it hard to identify and taken sincerely and seriously, or to what group of people this term is applied. They can be manipulative and exploitive. However, all narcissists are not alike.

Malignant Narcissists seek to dominate others and can be abusive and destructive. They lack any conscience and find joy in the damage that they cause. The Malignant Narcissist can be, by far, the most damaging. They tend to demonstrate a darker side to their self-centeredness, beyond just wanting primarily to focus on themselves and be admired and held in extremely high regard by all who know them.

This narcissistic type wants to get their own way and doesn't care who they hurt in the process. They view the world in black and white and see others as their friend or their competition which, in their mind equals foe. They don't care about the pain they cause others and they seek to win at all costs. They may also have a sadistic streak as well as antisocial traits. Some behaviorists feel there is little difference between psychopaths and malignant narcissists.

There are other types of narcissists that fall into some of the categories. They are not major but bear some of their characteristics.

Malignant Narcissistic Boss – It´s sad for anyone who has this type of boss. Unfortunately, there are many in senior management and leaders whose personalities support narcissistic traits. Working under this type of narcissist can be hellish and for many, the only way to deal with it is to get another job if they can. Research has shown that in leadership there is a darker underside and it frequently comes when power falls into the hands of people who develop a desire for it.

A culture of "yes" staff is frequently headed by management executives who impose their narcissism into the organization's culture. Narcissism in the workplace is needed in some way because if an organization lacks it there is no leadership, no path to creativity and no self-esteem in the organization's culture.

However, when narcissism turns into a personality disorder it can manifest itself into malignant narcissists at the helm that often decimates organizations and then leave to move on to the next. The organization had become one of "yes" regardless of how it affected the organization's culture because the malignant narcissist did not want to hear anything but that.

Vindictive Narcissist – Can fall under the Malignant Narcissist. This narcissist will set out to destroy another person who challenges them. If they are challenged (and the other person doesn't even realize what they've done) they will have an obsessive need to see the other declared the loser by going on a destructive rampage. The challenge can be the slightest and once provoked will stop at nothing to be destructive. They will lie about the other person, talk trash to friends and family about them, possibly aim at getting them fired.

Chapter 3:
Empaths and Narcissists

W orking on your relationship helps you realize who you are and your role. Are you acting like your true self with your partner? Do you understand how you act, and are you sensitive to what another person needs so much that you try to feel what they are feeling?

Sometimes, our relationships teach us the most significant lessons so that we can achieve a greater sense of self, through growth and loving who we are. It is possible within a healthy partnership. However, it is challenging and requires a lot more attention to the details with a narcissistic relationship.

The partners of those in a narcissistic relationship are often in a codependent attitude because it is the only way to have a balance. Therefore, the toxic patterns and loops continue and don't stop unless someone leaves or decides to make a change.

Empaths are individuals with an interesting and unique set of skills. They can develop in early life and are often misconstrued as overly sensitive, having learning difficulties, being emotionally challenged, delicate, or intense. Empaths are just highly sensitive to other people's energies, needs, and unspoken feelings. Some empaths are so connected to someone else's problems or emotional states that they absorb it into their reality and begin to feel as the other person is feeling.

The main sign that you could be an empath is that you will absorb or take in another person's or group of people's emotions, and sometimes, their physical feelings or symptoms. An empath is highly sensitive and intuitive and will filter the world around them through their inherent capabilities. It is hard for some empaths to verbally express or intellectualize what they are feeling because it is not always their emotion that they are feeling.

Being an empath can be very overwhelming. If you don't know how to clear other people's energies from your experiences, you can end up carrying around a lot of other people's feelings which can lead to some of the following issues:

- Depression

- Anxiety

- Panic attacks

- Chronic fatigue

- Stressful feelings

- Paranoia

- Self-doubt

- Chronic worry

- Binges (food, sex, drugs, etc.)

- Physical symptoms or illness

Understanding the common traits of an empath may help you better understand why they are often inclined to become involved with a narcissistic person in the first place. Here are some of the most common traits of being an empath:

Highly Sensitive

Being very nurturing, attentive, good listeners, spiritually open, and givers, empaths have a lot of heart and urge to give it to people. They are very supportive and ready to drop what they are doing to help you in a time of need. Empaths can also be easily hurt, emotionally, and mentally, because they are so open and receptive.

Emotionally Absorbent

Because they are so highly in tune with other people's feelings and emotional moods, whether they are good or bad, empaths will feel these extremes because of how easily they can absorb those emotions. They can absorb another's anxiety, rage, and depression, which, in the end, is exhausting. They can also absorb love and pleasure, joy and happiness, and can feel that flourish as well.

Naturally Introverted

Because of how easily they can absorb other people's energy, emotions, and physical pain and are highly sensitive to all things around them, being in large groups, loud spaces, or crowds can amplify all of this, making it hard for the empath to find pleasure in that experience. They can be more introverted, choosing to have more time alone, or in small groups, or one-on-one contact. Some empaths are more extroverted but will still require ample time apart to "recharge" their energy.

Highly Intuitive

The empath tends to experience life through intuition, rather than critical thinking. They can have a strong gut reaction to something or avoid their intuition, which causes greater problems later. The empath needs to develop their intuition.

Overwhelmed in Relationships

Because an empath may need more alone time to recover from their sensitivities and intuitive gifts, some relationships can be complicated, especially if their partner requires more "togetherness." It is easy for an empath to be engulfed by someone else because of how easily they can absorb someone else's energy. So, they can experience a different set of challenges while in a relationship with a partner.

Over-Giving

An empath is often in danger of over giving out of a desire to help others in pain. An empath doesn't just offer solace; they take it on and make it their problem too because of an innate desire to aid and help others. In relationships, this can create a toxic imbalance.

Understanding these traits can help you understand some of the dynamic qualities of being an empath and why that could translate into a relationship with someone narcissistic. The empath will work hard to love, help, and intuitively connect with their partner, but it is a toxic cycle from the very beginning.

A Toxic Attraction

Narcissists and empaths have a tendency to be drawn together. A narcissist will thrive and feel most content while being adored by another. The empath presents a lot of compassion and understanding that will be offered freely within a bond of love or relationship. As such, the empath will take on the role of forgiveness, enabling the narcissist to persist in their determination to be admired and worshipped.

The narcissist will idealize the empath in the partnership as being a truly "perfect mate" because of how loving, kind, and attentive they are, however, over time, when the empath has questions or desires to help the narcissist through their issues, the narcissist will stop idealizing their partner, and then begin to accuse them of being the problem, not them.

There is a huge difference between these two types of people: empaths have empathy, narcissists do not. Now, you can see why this is not a good relationship and how it can quickly become toxic.

Narcissists have a lot of tactics to manipulate the empath in their relationship. Because an empath is so forgiving and understanding, accepting the flaws and personal growth of another, they are willing to offer a chance, giving space to their partner, and hearing them out without judgment.

A narcissist will use an act of love or thoughtful words as an incentive or to "pay for" the love they are requiring or demanding, which isn't love at all: it's manipulation. An empath may have a hard time seeing this because all they want to do is help their partner grow and to be a supportive and loving friend.

This kind of back and forth, the loop of mental and emotional abuse, manipulation, and conditional loving can cause a traumatic bond that fuses the empath to the narcissist, making it feel difficult to leave the relationship (codependency).

The empath will begin to feel incapable, unworthy, defective. It will start to question their flaws, ability to love well, and even their identity as a person, all because of the trauma of manipulation caused by narcissistic abuse.

Having empathy and being an empath is not a bad thing in any relationship. It requires that you have an apparent understanding of how other people can affect you emotionally, mentally, and physically.

Now that you have an understanding about empaths and narcissists, you can move forward to discover more about the relationship patterns of a narcissist in general.

Chapter 4:
Narcissism in Relationships

N arcissistic relationships are very toxic and can cause many effects on the victims. Many narcissistic relationships start as normal relationships. The narcissist targets an individual they deem ideal for personal glorification or any other motive. In many cases, a narcissist will target a person they think well enough for self-glorification. In all types of relationships, is it friendship or sexual relationship, the approach used by narcissists is the same.

They spot an ideal person, whom they idealize as the right person to fulfill their objectives. As we have mentioned above, narcissists are obsessed with having the best things in life. They enjoy associating with the most successful personalities in life to impose their superiority over everyone else. As the narcissist looks for a victim to achieve his/her agenda, they look for a person that will make them look superior.

After spotting the victim, the narcissist will devise a plan to lure the victim. For romantic relationships, the narcissist may present a personality that is charming and sweet. At first, anyone can fall for a narcissist. They sweep in with all types of charming romantic gestures. Although it may look like love at first, what they feel is an obsession. They are obsessed with owning their target, so they use charm to attract the victim. If it is a man, he will target the most beautiful girl and treat her like a queen. He will use every means possible to win her over.

He may call her regularly or buy her good gifts. Narcissists may use a lot of money to win their target relationship partners. If it is friendship, narcissists also invest in creating intimacy. They go to places where their target victim hangout. They may use a lot of money to impress their target victim. They may buy gifts or even take them out for drinks. At this stage, they make sure they win the trust and love of their victims. Because they are so sweet and charming, narcissists are hard to resist. The victims slowly find themselves deep in love with the narcissist.

After winning over their ideal person, the narcissists start revealing their real personalities. At this stage, the victim is already in love and cannot make a sound judgment. The abuser begins showing their true characters one by one. It is difficult for the victims to read the signs because these individuals are very strategic. At some point, they are usually in love with the victim. They may even be in love with the victim for over a decade. During the time they are in love, narcissists are very obsessive.

They will do anything to have the person they love around them. They may go to all extends to prove their love, even crying tears or threatening to commit suicide. Victims may not easily see the red flags because narcissists hide their identity underneath. When the true characters start popping up, slowly. It starts with verbal abuses, which may sound harmless in the beginning. They may use verbal or physical abuse. Sometimes sexual abuses may crop in, but they will show remorse afterward and apologize. The apologies are filled with tears and begging. Because narcissists are attached to their victims, they will do anything to gain forgiveness, but it does not take long before they repeat the same mistake.

When the victim eventually starts realizing the true character of a narcissistic person, the abuser changes the approach. A narcissist starts using manipulation and blackmail to maintain the relationship. At first, the narcissist uses deception in the name of romance to start the relationship. They may put on a fake personality that is charming to lure their victims. However, as soon as the partners start getting acquainted with each other, the true personality comes out. It is difficult for a narcissist to maintain the lies for a long time.

Most narcissists would maintain a fake personality for as long as it works for thcm. However, the unfortunate part is that lies don't last. As soon as two people get intimate, all the lies start showing up. The true personality of the narcissist starts coming out. They start reacting violently and aggressively when angered. They start showing dominance and the constant need to be in control. Narcissists change their perception over a person they showed love and start looking at her or him as an object. They start treating their victim as a tool and worthless. Their idealized personality of being superior to all human beings starts showing.

Causes of Narcissism in Relationships

The Need to Be Dominant

Narcissistic partners start showing their true personalities when they want to take control and dominate. If a narcissistic partner realizes that the other partner is equal or dominant, he/she starts using abuse to dominate.

The Need to Control

Narcissism behavior crops when the narcissistic partner wants to have control over finances, assets, and children. A narcissistic partner will do anything possible to gain absolute control.

The Need to Be Loved

A narcissistic partner does not believe he/she can be rejected. The narcissist will do anything possible to be loved even when the love runs out. Such partners may start employing violence and intimidation to force the other party to show love.

The Need to Maintain Perfection

Narcissistic individuals are perfectionists and do not believe in failure. If cracks in a marriage may lead to divorce, the person may get abusive and manipulative to maintain a perfect family image. Narcissists will not allow the other partner to introduce imperfection into their life.

Financial Gain

Partners may turn narcissistic to gain finances and assets. If the property and assets belong to one partner, the other partner may do everything possible to control the finances.

Need to Control the Children

Narcissists use children to achieve their goals. A narcissist in a relationship may turn against their partner to have children on their side. They eventually brainwash the children and paint the other parent as a villain.

Consequences of Narcissism in Relationships

Broken Trust

The victims of narcissistic abuse in a relationship lose trust in humanity. They eventually grow paranoid and look at everyone as an abuser. They do not trust friends, family, or anybody who tries to move close to them. Narcissistic abuse victims may never trust another partner in life even after healing from the many emotional scars.

Physical and Emotional Injury

Narcissism in a relationship eventually results in emotional and physical abuse. The abuses may cause injuries that may be long-lasting. Emotional injuries take years to heal and may develop other mental conditions in the victim. Victims of narcissistic abuse may suffer from stress or anxiety.

Broken Relationships

Narcissists ensure that they separate their victims from friends and families. Being in a narcissistic relationship for a long time may lead to a loss of friends and family. If the abuse continues for long before rescue, the victim may not be able to have relationships with family or even his/ her children.

Damaged Public Image

Narcissists spread rumors to finish off someone's personality. They will spread lies and ensure that everyone paints the victims the villain. After a long time, a person in a narcissistic relationship might never be able to recover again. He/she loses the trust of other people. The victim is often left alone and unable to cope with the situation.

Bankruptcy

Narcissists exploit every way to ensure that their victims do not have any weapon left. They will use sabotage to ensure that victims lose their jobs. Narcissists will blackmail their victims and try to take anything they own. They may commit fraud, theft, and even get in debts using the name of the victim. The victim is left bankrupt. The victim may not have a credible personality to find a job. They are usually into many debts and unable to secure a loan on of any kind.

Poor Health

The victims of narcissistic abuse often end up being unhealthy. They are treated in an inhumane manner and may lose weight due to poor eating habits. They may also suffer from sexually transmitted diseases since most narcissistic partners are polygamous. They engage in multiple relationships without hiding and transfer sexually transmitted infections to their partners without regret.

Low Self-Esteem

Victims of narcissistic relationships suffer from low self-esteem for a long time. Few manage to heal completely. Many years of verbal abuse and demining words eventually take root in the mind of a person. The victim may eventually believe that they are not worthy of being loved or cared for. Victims are unable to believe in their talents or capabilities.

Anxiety

Individuals who are in narcissistic relationships live in constant fear. Even if they come out, the fear never goes away. They are always afraid of upsetting their narcissistic partners. They fear the consequences. They are made to understand that their narcissistic partner is omnipresent. They are always looking over their shoulders when doing anything. They lack privacy and cannot have a private life.

Regret and Self-Blame

Eventually, any individual who has been in a narcissistic relationship blames themselves for letting such a person have control. They end up believing that they are stupid, and that is why someone else had total control over their minds. They do not know that anyone could be a victim of narcissistic relationships.

Chapter 5:
Stages of a Narcissistic Relationship

T he main reason for getting into a relationship is to connect, love, and share with another person. A narcissist's reason for getting into a relationship differs significantly. They are incapable of love, so the typical romantic bond is not possible.

More than any other person, narcissists need people. They need people to keep their sense of being, self-worth, and self-esteem up. There is this void present in the narcissists that can only be filled by the love and admiration of others. It is what they care about. This is what prompts them to enter a relationship. They are not after caring for you or sharing your joy and pain. When they see anyone that can be a source for them, they will go to any means to make this person fall for them, even if it means putting up a false perception.

The relationship with a narcissist follows four phases.

Love-Bombing Stage

One of the motivations of a narcissist in choosing a partner is what they can get from them. That is why they often go after rich people, people with class and influence, people with attractive bodies, etc.

Once they have their target, a narcissist directs all their effort and energy in chasing the victim. They are so meticulous in their pursuit that they project the image the victim craves for. It is like a little boy that becomes obsessed with a shiny new bicycle. He annoys his parents so much they have no choice but to get him the bike. On reaching the bicycle, this boy rides it every day, and any spare moment he has is on the toy. He goes everywhere with the bike. After a couple of weeks, he is fed up and wants a new toy.

They will bombard their target with so much love, and it seems they idolize them. The narcissists will share all their hopes and dreams with you freely and seem interested in yours. Unfortunately, however, the victim often gets carried away to get so convinced they have found a life-partner. Remember what the narcissists does majorly is mirror what they know appeals to their target. This convinces the target without a doubt that this person is for them.

They are so carried away in this euphoria that what comes next meets them is a shock.

The Devaluation Stage

For most narcissists, the love-bombing stage lasts between a couple of weeks to a few months. All they need is enough time to be sure you are already entangled in their web; you are head over heels in love and committed to them. Unfortunately, many targets are clueless because all they are seeing is the narcissist with a mask of what appeals to them. This is the phase where they show their true colors.

This stage begins slowly and subtly at first. Their commitment, faithfulness will die down. They become moody, stop returning your calls, getting irritated quickly at what you say or do. You get confused, thinking it is something you said or did. They were supposed to be in love with you, why would they treat you this bad?

The reason is to have total control over you.

Narcissist's aim of mistreating their victim is to gradually destroy themselves in yourself and others, your self-worth, and self-esteem. Their behavior and attitude get so cruel that it leaves you bewildered. A partner is supposed to be supportive and loving, but suddenly it seems like a switch flipped and transformed. Nothing you do is ever appreciated, and they even call you as clingy if you try to maintain the normal amount of commitment and passion that you once shared.

Narcissists tend to get bored with people easily, which usually starts in their heads. They start telling themselves there was nothing special about you after all. The slightest provocation will set them off, and they will lash out at you strongly. They are never present, and even when they are, their minds are miles away. As the narcissist withdraws, the partner in a bid to keep the fire burning clings in demand for his attention. However, all your clinging only drives him further away and even gets him angry. Their target takes the blame and criticism for everything that goes wrong.

This often wrecks the partner emotionally. What on earth could have happened to their supposed "soul mate?" What many victims do not realize is that the veil is just falling off. It is the person behind the veil that they are just meeting. However, they try desperately to find the person they fell in love with, with no avail. Unknown to them, this person never existed. They were only victims of the narcissist manipulation to secure their supply.

Any ill-treatment the narcissist caused you don't bother them. They were never capable of forming healthy bonding in the first place. All you experienced was a facade.

At this stage, they have succeeded in making you scramble for their love. This way, you try with all you might to please them and succumb to their demands, with the hope that the person you fell in love with comes back.

They might resort to criticizing everything about you. It could be your friends and loved ones. They will make you uncomfortable in front of your family and loved ones, so you begin to avoid them. Not only that, but they will also always find fault in your appearance. If it does not appeal to them, if it makes you outshine them, they will criticize and condemn it.

At this stage, either of two things will happen; your narcissist partner might have found a new target and directed all their attention on them, making them ignore you. Or you decide you are done with the games and end it, bringing in the third phase.

The Discard Stage

To the narcissist, you are only a pawn. You are only relevant to the narcissist because they used you to fulfill a need. As soon as the need is fulfilled, they will discard you faster than an old newspaper. The ease with which a narcissist pulls away from their partner once their usefulness is exhausted is alarming. Many people will ask themselves over and over:

- Did I mean anything to him?

- Did he even care about me?

The brutal answer is, No. the narcissists are not capable of love and emotions. You were just a source of power for them. You were only relevant if they could feed from you. Once they have had enough of you, you will be shoved off the pedestal without mercy and warning.

Any attempt to oppose them will be met with strict resistance, and if you are dealing with a brutal one, they can go as far as destroying you. Remember, you never meant anything to them, so they will not think twice before leaving. They only care about a single individual in the entire world, which is themselves.

The Return

If you manage to get this stage of a narcissistic relationship, you are free. By this time, the narcissist is out of your house. Even though it is hard and tough at first, you will improve. The storm is over, and your life will be calmer and smoother with less stress. This is the stage where you need to start looking after yourself. All the energy you directed at supporting and caring for your ex should be directed at taking care of yourself.

Chapter 6:
Narcissistic Abuse

N arcissistic individuals exhibit various types of behavior, with some constituting psychological and emotional abuse. It is essential to have an understanding of some of the types of narcissistic abuse for one to know if they are being subjected to such abuse. Although there are many forms of narcissistic abuse, some of the most common types of abuse include: intimidation, trivializing, isolation, restraint, aggression, and endangerment. All types of narcissistic abuse can have very significant effects on the people involved. They result in the abuser feeling that they have the upper hand while the victim is made to feel belittled and that their opinions do not matter.

Intimidation

Intimidation is one of the most popular forms of abuse, and it entails instilling a sense of fear on the other person. For instance, a narcissistic person will use fear to manipulate another person to do something exactly the way they want. In a relationship, a narcissistic partner can threaten to leave unless the other partner agrees to specific predetermined terms that they have put in place. Intimidation in any form can undermine the quality of any relationship, whether intimate or otherwise. A good example would be employees who only seem to go out of their way to work hard because their employer constantly threatens to fire them. Such employees will most certainly end up disliking their employer and will quit the company as soon another job opportunity comes along.

Intimidation constitutes a direct threat. A look at some of the other forms of narcissistic abuse reveals that most of them do not constitute a direct threat. For instance, a person might endanger the life of another without making an immediate demand from them in terms of it is that they want. However, when it comes to intimidation, the threat is direct. Intimidation or bullying usually takes the form of asking someone to do something and offering a stern warning that failure to do so will result in severe consequences. The main goal of intimidation, just as is the case with the other forms of narcissistic abuse, is to make someone feel obliged to do something on account of possible dire consequences on their part in case they fail to do so.

Intimidation may also be applied based on the behavior of the person in question. For example, someone may request you into something but with a look on their face that seems to say, 'you better do this or else you will deeply regret.' Implied intimidation might have consequences that could be as severe as an expressed intimidation.

Trivializing

In addition to intimidation, the second form of narcissistic abuse is trivializing. When you trivialize the thoughts or ideas of another person, you make them feel less important. For example, a colleague might come up with a good idea of how the company can make more money, but for one reason or the other, you come up with another suggestion that seems to undermine the viability of the idea put forward by your colleague. In case you are doing so deliberately, then you might be exhibiting signs of narcissistic abuse.

The main objective of a narcissist is to make another person feel inferior while uplifting themselves. Constant trivializing of the ideas expressed by other people is considered one of the main forms of narcissistic personality disorder. It diminishes the overall self-esteem of the other person making the person with the personality disorder feel superior. For instance, when someone tells you do not have what it takes to achieve a certain objective. They are trying to dissuade you from trying since they know that if you try, the chances are that you may end up succeeding and become more 'important' than them, which happens to be their greatest fear.

Aggression

Aggression is also another form of narcissistic behavior. Aggression in this context refers to being unnecessary angry towards another person. Anger within the mindset of a person with a narcissistic personality is seen as a tool that can be used to control another person, especially if they want to manipulate them to behave in a certain manner. Aggressive behavior and anger can take the shape of someone over-reacting to a mundane situation. The narcissistic person might, for instance, be unapproachable for days because someone has done something that is against their wishes.

There are many shapes that anger can take. At times, it might involve the silent treatment whereby one partner ends not talking to the other for extended periods. Similarly, anger can also involve yelling or swearing to another person. Loud yelling to another person is usually meant to make them feel powerless and more inclined to abide by the wishes of the person with the disorder. This is what makes it a form of abuse concerning narcissistic personality disorder.

Endangerment

When you endanger someone, you are putting them in unsafe situations that can potentially threaten their lives. Endangerment is considered a form of abuse as far as the narcissistic individual is concerned. The end game is to make another person feel so insecure and thus give in to your demands.

Endangerment can take two forms, and these are direct and indirect endangerment. Direct endangerment involves threatening the life of someone that you want to gain control of. For instance, a narcissistic person might want to ensure that all shareholders of a company vote in a certain manner. To do this, the person may opt to send life-threatening emails to all shareholders to influence their voting decisions. This is a form of direct endangerment since it threatens the life of the affected individual. Indirect endangerment, on the other hand, usually involves threatening the lives of the people around the target person. For instance, one might threaten to kidnap the child of someone to influence their behavior.

Stalking

Stalking is also another form of endangerment is that entails following another person with a view of making them feel scared. In some cases, the stalker might end up no harm, but, in many cases, stalkers have been known to attack the person who they are stalking physically. No matter the form of endangerment exhibited by a narcissistic individual, this behavior is deemed abusive because it tends to influence another person's behavior unduly.

In some cases, the stalker's objective might seem innocent, as is the case with celebrities. Such stalkers are usually obsessed with the person in question, and so they try to be as close to them as possible. They might end up breaking into the house of the person they are interested in, hanging around their car while they are away to feel close to that person. Be that as it may, all forms of stalking are narcissistic behavior. This is because the stalker is concerned with their own needs, which may be to threaten the other person or to feel close to them. The stalker is unmoved by the fact that their behavior can result in fear and extreme discomfort on the part of the person they are pursuing. This underscores their narcissistic personality.

Verbal Abuse

Verbal abuse refers to the use of harsh and abusive language on other people. Verbal abuse is also a form of narcissistic abuse commonly employed with this form of personality disorder. Many people who use abusive language tend to make the other person feel insecure about themselves and their capabilities. For instance, someone might refer to you as 'stupid' or an 'idiot' even though they know that that is not the case.

However, you might end up feeling that you do not have what it takes to attain a certain objective because of the abusive words thrown your way by the narcissistic person.

Verbal abuse is usually considered a form of extreme narcissistic behavior on the part of the perpetrator. This is because it is a direct abuse involving the use of abusive words designed to undermine another person's self-esteem. Furthermore, many people who are subjected to verbal abuse end up staying with the narcissistic person since they do not even have the confidence and much-needed self-esteem that will allow them to move onto the next relationship.

Master manipulation credentials of narcissistic people have made it much easier for them to embrace this form of abuse. They will use it against you whenever they want something from or simply when they need to make you feel small while elevating themselves. It is also important to note that narcissistic individuals will also want you to go down to their level by prompting an abusive response from you. For this reason, you should never give in to the trap. Instead of replying with abusive words, it is advisable to maintain your calm and try to put your point across with uttermost restraint. By doing so, you will end up revealing them for who they really are, and this will negate their ill objectives.

Sadistic Behavior

Sadism means to delight in the pain or misfortune of other people. Many people who are narcissists also exhibit sadistic behavior. This implies that such people are happy when others are in pain. For instance, they may find some abnormal joy from your physical pain occasioned by an illness. Similarly, a narcissist can also find happiness in your emotional pain occasioned by the loss of a job or failure to attain a personal goal.

Sadism is considered a form of extreme anti-social behavior that can morph into many things. For a person with a narcissistic personality disorder, their tendency towards sadism can make them take proactive steps in instigating your pain. For example, they may orchestrate your downfall in your career or workplace to derive some joy in your unfortunate experience.

It is important to remember that narcissism and narcissistic abuse is perpetrated by people who are insecure about themselves. These people will want to establish control over you, influence how you think to intimidate you, and at times, hurt you. Their overall goal is for them to remain superior over you to mask their insecurity. However, with this knowledge and understanding, you can flip the script quite literally. This is because; you will know how to behave around such people so as not to empower them. For instance, you can recognize when someone uses anger, intimidation, and abusive words as tools to influence your thinking. You can choose not to give in to their manipulative ways, such as not spending too much time doubting yourself just because someone called you an idiot. By doing so, you will end up thriving in life and attaining your true potential, thus negating the narcissist people's objectives.

Chapter 7:
Narcissistic Abuse Syndrome

This syndrome leaves an injured individual broken. It has a few names, including Trauma Associated Narcissistic Symptoms (TANS) and Post Traumatic Narcissism Syndrome (PTNS). Individuals with this syndrome feel mortified because their abusers constrained the shame onto them and may create Stockholm Syndrome. Their abusers controlled them with the goal that they structure tight emotional bonds. The syndrome clarifies why victims have a convincing need to remain in their relationships, notwithstanding the abuse.

Victims experience flashbacks of the abuse. They may have a fear for their security and become particularly anxious. They may experience issues coming to choices, expand affectability, and check their surroundings for dangers, to such an extent that their conduct gets enthusiastic. Wretchedness, fractiousness, and blame usually go with their anxiety. Victims may encounter these sentiments so unequivocally that they may hurt themselves and be unsociable.

Narcissistic Stockholm Syndrome

Stockholm syndrome is a fascinating phenomenon, and it's when adults being abused by their captors begin to experience positive feelings towards the same people abusing them. Over time, the captives develop gratefulness whenever their captor shows them some sign of approval or the tiniest gesture of generosity if you can call it that. The captives even bond with their captors and love them on top of that. The captives become like children, dependent on whatever the captors dictate to them, believing they ought to do whatever they can to make their captors happy.

At the start of the relationship or friendship with the narcissist, they want to get their hooks into you. So, they begin by giving you a lot of rewards. Were the rewards for the rats was food; in your case, it was all the love, attention, romantic gestures, and sweet nothings in your ear. The narcissist will make sure you know you're an amazing, wonderful person. She will get you the most exquisite and thoughtful gifts, give you experiences that are out of this world, and do whatever is necessary to make you feel special.

Once you understand the way the narcissist works with them, you'll be able to understand better why you can't leave a narcissist easily. It's only natural for anyone getting that much love and attention to come to love it. It also helps when it's someone attractive who has taken it upon themselves to massage your ego. When it's the narcissist doing this, it's anything but innocent. This is the love-bombing phase we've covered, which is designed to get you hooked.

The narcissist teaches you to get all the love, attention, and validation you could ever need by looking to them alone. Now they've taught you on where to get the food they're confident you're not going to look elsewhere; he stops feeding you all the time. Here is where the narcissist makes sure whatever positive rewards, they give you, come because you do things which please the narcissist. You don't realize that you're working a bit harder to get the food you want. You're being programmed by the narcissist to keep making efforts to keep them happy, whether you get rewarded each time.

The narcissist kicks things up by not just denying you the approval and love you crave, but by treating you like crap. The criticism grows. They're more demanding, more controlling. They'll embarrass you in public, to keep you in your place. Now and then, they will give you a nice reward, but it will be completely random. The one thing that does stay constant is that there are more terrible times than happy times.

You'll wonder why any of this is going on. Trust that your narcissist will give you the perfect answer: You're the issue. The only way to fix things is for you to do more of this or less of that.

Once you agree to everything, your narcissist wants. The narcissist now has complete control of you. This is where you, the captive, begin to feel positive about this robber of joy and all things good. You allow yourself to become like a child, trusting and relying on them to make the best decisions for you because, as far as you're concerned, you can't do anything right, and they're there to save you. At this point, you're resigned to your fate. You live each day fueled only by the hope that they will show you some kindness someday.

Now you're all about getting that approval. It doesn't matter that they abuse you. You still want them to be in your life. It scares you to death just thinking of them abandoning you for someone else, and you've become bonded with them through the constant trauma.

At the first sign that you're about to leave them, the narcissist will suddenly switch up. They will do and say whatever they need to, so you remain with them. This is the hoover maneuver. It often starts small, and then they will head right back to where it all started. They start to make you promises about how they are going to change, or they're going for therapy and tell you things will be better this time. They tell you also how much they love you, need you, and life is not worth it.

You are tempted to give in to the hoover maneuver since the narcissist was so careless with your feelings since they humiliated you and hurt you endlessly, only to discard you mercilessly, you have a lot of vested interested in the relationship. It becomes hard to take that all that pain, shame, and blame could all have been for nothing. You refuse to accept that the time you spent together was a pointless, meaningless waste. So, you want to try again and see if you can both make it work. The abuse starts again, and the cycle continues.

Signs You're the Victim of a Narcissist

You're Depressed

It's difficult to remain positive when your accomplice persistently puts you down. If you don't encounter anything, however, negligence and cynicism, chances are you're in a condition of misery.

Indications of sadness include:

- Feeling miserable and shameful

- Loss of intrigue

- Heightened anxiety

- Problems dozing and weariness

- Irritability

- Changes in weight

Misery can send you into an emotional and mental down winding. Your partner lowers your self-esteem.

Narcissists Are Known for Bringing Down the Self-Esteem of Others

By having low self-esteem, your accomplice can deal with you. If you feel lesser than your accomplice, it's a lot simpler to control you.

If your self-worth has endured a shot, you likely feel as though you can't get away from this terrible reality.

Nothing You Do Is Enough

Regardless of what you do, it's rarely enough. By corrupting and disparaging you, your accomplice picks up a favorable position.

You Are Convinced You Are Going Crazy

A narcissist will say and effectively make you feel as though your musings aren't right. At the point when you begin to pick up lucidity of the circumstance, your accomplice will persuade you that it's all in your mind. This method is known as gaslighting. Your accomplice will deliberately make you feel as though you are losing your marbles. Gaslighting enables your accomplice to increase significantly more control.

It's Impossible to Leave

You've set aside an effort to consider it thoroughly. You've talked everything through with a dear companion. Similarly, as you're prepared to leave, your accomplice pulls you back in.

Narcissists are specialists at stretching their accomplices as far as possible. The minute you choose you've had enough; your accomplice transforms into a wad of appeal. You get all the affection and consideration when you need to leave. In any case, when you remain, you're disregarded.

Chapter 8:
Narcissist and Codependency

The narcissist rarely has trouble drawing people in, but this is not solely due to the narcissist's charm. Some people are much more vulnerable to narcissistic abuse than others. Narcissists are skilled at recognizing and targeting these people.

The prime characteristic the narcissist is looking for is codependency, the self-destructive urge to take a caregiver role even if it harms you. Narcissists sometimes get in relationships with other narcissists, but a narcissist will often partner with a codependent person.

The leading cause of codependency is childhood trauma, which is also the cause of narcissism. In fact, the two conditions are broadly similar and can be interpreted as different attempts to solve the same underlying problem. A child who cannot develop a stable sense of self looks for the person in the reactions of others. Narcissism and codependency are two different ways of doing that.

Codependent behavior can be described as narcissistic in some circumstances. For instance, a mother who focuses on her children to the exclusion of everything else in her life might be described as codependent, since she defines herself solely by her self-sacrificing caregiver behavior. However, it's easy to use caregiving as a manipulative strategy, especially when combined with guilt-tripping and emotional blackmail, in which case the behavior is essentially narcissistic.

Some therapists consider narcissism to be a type of codependency, as the narcissist is just as dependent on the opinions of others and often for the same reasons. One person can be narcissistic in some relationships and codependent in others. For example, a mother whose attitude to her children is narcissistic can still function as a codependent caregiver to an alcoholic husband. The difference is simply that the codependent person is the giver in the relationship while the narcissist is the taker, yet both parties need each other to play out the roles they feel compelled to play.

The Symptoms of Codependency

Unlike narcissism, codependency is not a diagnosed personality disorder. However, codependency does have a set of recognizable characteristics or symptoms, including:

- Weak boundaries between self and other, a tendency to internalize and take responsibility for other people's emotions.

- A deep sense of inner shame or inadequacy.

- Poor self-esteem.

- Difficulty saying "no," and an urge to please others even when it causes you harm.

- A powerful need to take care of someone or a feeling of worthlessness unless other people need you.

- Poor communication skills or reluctance to say what you're feeling.

- Inability to clearly articulate your own needs.

- Obsessively thinking about and analyzing your relationships with others.

- A tendency to react with intense emotion to any judgment or criticism.

- The urge to control other people and make their decisions for them.

- Denial of your needs in favor of meeting the needs of others.

- Fear of emotional intimacy.

- Perfectionism.

- Inability to be alone, causing intense depression when you are not in a relationship.

- A strong need to be recognized for all your sacrifices, leading to resentment when you don't feel appreciated.

- A feeling that you are unworthy of love, or that you are a failure.

- Fear of abandonment.

- Denial of the problem.

The codependent person is driven by a deep inner wound to seek for love and validation but believes herself to be unworthy of the love she seeks. This drives her to prove herself through extravagant self-sacrifice, putting the other person's needs above her own. When her self-destructive people-pleasing is not appreciated, she becomes resentful and passive-aggressive. However, she finds it almost impossible to break the relationship off due to her fear of being alone.

The relationship between a narcissist and a codependent person is not just a simple matter of abuser and victim. The narcissistic abuser needs someone to put him first, and the codependent person needs to put someone first. In theory, these needs could be compatible. However, the narcissist's basic lack of empathy poisons the dynamic. No matter how much self-sacrifice the codependent offers, the narcissist will never reciprocate with gratitude and appreciation. Instead, the narcissist will project his self-loathing onto his codependent partner while remaining self-centered and entitled. The only possible result is misery for both.

How Does Codependency Develop?

Role reversal is one of the most common childhood experiences that can cause codependency later in life. Role reversal happens whenever the child is asked to play the role of the parent. If a parent is unable to take care of themselves due to illness, substance abuse, or mental health problems, the child may step in and take over the caregiver role.

Sometimes, this role is forced on the child by a dysfunctional parent. Still, there are also cases where it happens as an unavoidable consequence of a serious illness and a lack of support from outside the household. Either way, it's deeply harmful to a child to take on the parental role. The child often develops a compulsive need to be the caregiver in every relationship, along with intense but buried resentment for having been forced into such a demanding role at such an early age. The martyr-like qualities of the codependent come from this paradoxical combination of resentment and self-sacrificing altruism.

A child who lives in an abusive household may learn to associate love and approval with successfully pleasing the abusive parent and avoiding their often-unpredictable anger. This pattern of self-negation and people-pleasing can develop into codependency if the child retains the capacity for empathy, or develops into narcissism if the capacity for empathy is lost. In both cases, the person sees love and acceptance as something that depends on how others perceive you. The difference between the two is that the codependent wants to make the other person happy and thus "earn" love and acceptance, while the narcissist wants to convince the other person that he "deserves" love and acceptance due to his superior qualities.

The Appeal of the Narcissist

What makes the narcissist so appealing to the codependent person is a combination of factors? The narcissist's apparent self-confidence can make him seem compelling and dynamic. The codependent person lacks a solid inner self, and the narcissist seems to have what she lacks. He doesn't, because his impressive persona is only a front. However, the codependent person has no way of knowing this and is drawn to a partner who seems to have what she's missing.

The codependent's need to serve others will ensure that she supplies the narcissist with what he wants, but the narcissist feels no need to continue supplying the affection and warmth the codependent needs. Now and then, the narcissist may start love-bombing the codependent again to keep her from leaving. This is especially likely after the narcissist's abusive and harmful behavior has pushed the codependent almost to the point of walking away. By turning the charm back on for a little while, the narcissist can fool the codependent into thinking things are getting better— for a little while. The rest of the time, he will take advantage of himself as fully entitled to what the codependent offers.

The toxic dynamic between the narcissist and the codependent becomes a cycle of abuse, which can be broken only when the narcissist moves on to a new source of narcissistic supply or when the codependent decides to break the cycle. Few if any narcissists will ever break the cycle on their own.

Codependents frequently engage in enabling behavior—that is, behavior that enables the other person to keep doing whatever destructive thing they've been doing without experiencing the consequences of that behavior.

A codependent person in a relationship with a narcissist might engage in any of the following behaviors:

- Minimizing or excusing the narcissist's abusive behavior.

- Keeping the narcissist's destructive actions private.

- Taking the blame or consequences for things the narcissist did.

- Paying debts that the narcissist incurred, such as debts from gambling or misusing credit.

- Participating in the abuser's triangulation strategies.

- Acting as the abuser's agent or "flying monkey" to re-victimize previous victims.

- Helping the narcissist hide criminal or immoral behavior from public knowledge.

- Giving the narcissist control over your finances.

These behaviors, though driven by the codependent's own need to take care of other people, only make it easier for the narcissist to continue the cycle of abuse and exploitation.

Chapter 9:
Emotional Manipulation

E motional manipulation can be unpretentious and misleading, leaving you bewildered and wobbly. They utilize these practices to get their direction or prevent you from saying or doing anything they don't care for. Or then again, it tends to be clear and requesting where fear, disgracing, and remorseful fits leave you shocked and immobilized.

Emotional manipulation isn't worthy, and the more you enable it to proceed, the more force and certainty the manipulator gains in this uneven relationship.

Emotional Manipulation Signs and Techniques

They Turn Your Words to Profit Them

The manipulator has trouble tolerating responsibility for their conduct. Regularly, on the off chance that you call them on it, they'll figure out how to turn it around to make you feel terrible or remorseful. For instance, you may submit an authentic question like, "It truly pesters me you didn't assist me with cleaning the house when you guaranteed you would."

Rather than saying 'sorry' recognizing their activities, and rectifying the circumstance, a manipulator will say something like, "You could never have requested that I help you on the off chance that you realized how overpowered I am. Why not consider me for once?"

They may offer a semi expression of remorse like, "Well, I'm extremely, unfortunately, I was working until late last evening. I realize I ought to have educated you regarding all the pressure I'm under and how tired I've been. I might be catching something."

This sort of manipulation is practically more regrettable than no conciliatory sentiment at all since it makes you feel awful for asking and anticipating that they should finish on something they guaranteed.

If a statement of regret feels fake or if the other individual answers with preventiveness or remorseful fits, don't enable them to pull off it. On the off chance that you do, it will simply engage them to do it once more. Clarify that a genuine statement of regret is unequivocal and followed by a conduct change.

The Manipulator Says Something and Later Denies It

A manipulator may express yes to a solicitation or pledge to you. Afterward, when the opportunity arrives to finish, they helpfully overlook they at any point said anything. Except if you have a chronicle of them making the guarantee, you can't generally demonstrate anything—so it's your "awful memory" against their lying words.

A gifted manipulator has a method for turning a past discussion or replaying it to suit their needs and make you feel like it's your shortcoming and neglectful, requesting, or strange. Emotional manipulation causes you to address yourself and make you feel awful or regretful that you tested the manipulator.

If you experience an example of these sleights of hand manipulation tactics in your relationship, start to record what the manipulator has guaranteed.

Emotional Manipulation Utilizes Remorseful Fits to Control You

This is definitive in manipulative conduct. "You proceed to the films without me. It's fine. I'll remain at home and finish the clothing."

"It's constantly about your needs. If you comprehended what sort of youth I had, you'd never request that I do that."

"If you truly need to go on the young ladies' end of the week, proceed. I simply don't see how you could leave the children for that long."

"I realize we can't bear to purchase another vehicle. In any case, I've never had another vehicle in my life. I surmise I'll simply live with this poop vehicle for eternity. I don't merit decent things."

The emotional manipulator realizes how to assume the unfortunate casualty job of flawlessness. They work up a pot of blame and compassion and serve it to you in loading ladleful.

They will say simply regarding anything to get their direction—particularly if they see a soft-hearted, sensitive injured individual.

You are not going insane. They are playing you for everything it has. Try not to succumb to these manipulatives, blame loaded trickeries. Try not to surrender to their latent requests or demands for compassion. This individual is a grown-up. Remind them of that, and how they are splendidly ready to adapt to your choice or activities.

Manipulators Attempt to Reduce Your Issues or Troubles

Emotional manipulators couldn't care less much about your significant issues—except if they can utilize them as a stage to feature their own. "You think you had it awful sitting in rush hour gridlock today? Did you ever consider how I need to manage traffic each day? It takes a very long time off my life. Be grateful you just needed to manage it today."

"Gosh, that is awful you and your mother fought. In any case, simply be grateful you have a mother. My mother is dead, and in any event, when she was alive, we fought substantially more than you and your mother do. It nearly felt like I never had a mother."

If you call attention to how the manipulator simply reversed the situation, they'll likely attempt to make you look selfish and forsaken. They won't recognize their narcissistic conduct or reframe the discussion around your agony or trouble.

There's very little you can do in these circumstances except for leave and discover another person who is more minding, humane, and develop. Try not to open your vulnerabilities to somebody who stomps on all over them.

They Utilize the Emotional, Controlling Secondary Passage Strategy

As opposed to being immediate and straightforward, manipulators will avoid legitimate correspondence and utilize aloof forceful techniques. They may talk despite your good faith with others, or ask another person to be their representative, so they don't need to be the troublemaker or young lady.

For instance, they may have a companion disclose to you they need to separate or make reference to your closest companion how miserable they are in the room.

They may utilize detached methods for telling you they're troubled or miserable by frowning, stepping, or giving the quiet treatment. Or on the other hand, they may state something strong; however, they act in extremely unsupportive manners.

For instance, your mate may state she's cheerful for you to complete a requesting work venture at home in the night times. However, she goes out shopping, leaving you home with the children.

For your very own significant serenity, get down on them about this conduct. More than likely, you'll get a cautious, angry response, however, at any rate, the manipulator sees that you realize what they're doing. Manipulative conduct happens consistently, it's the ideal opportunity to advise or think about your leave technique.

They Use Tactics That Suck the Energy Out of the Room

Manipulators have a method for strolling into a room and hauling a foreboding shadow alongside them. They need the consideration and spotlight to be on them, and they need to ensure everybody in the room sees if they are furious, troubled, or disappointed here and there.

Individuals will, in general, scramble to oblige the manipulator or to attempt to enable them "to feel much improved." They may ask, "Would you say you are OK? Is something incorrect?" This is only the opening the manipulator needs to bolster the compassion and energies of others. Being in the stay with a manipulator, a sensitive individual will feel depleted and cockeyed.

On the off chance that conceivable, leave the room. Why part with your energy and positive mind-set to a manipulator? In case you're stuck in the room, imagine yourself encompassed by an impervious hindrance that shields you from the negative vibes of the manipulator.

Emotional Manipulators Use Hostility or Outrage

Emotional manipulators regularly attempt to threaten others with forceful language, unpretentious dangers, or inside and out indignation. Particularly if they see you're awkward with showdown, they will utilize it to control you and get their direction rapidly. The objective is to encourage fear or extraordinary uneasiness so you'll paunch up rapidly. Possibly your significant other has a hissy fit each time you raise her over-spending. Your better half raises his voice and hammers entryways when you accomplish something he doesn't care for. After some time, the manipulator adapts all the person needs to get somewhat insane, and things will go their direction.

Except if you fear physical viciousness, get down on them about this conduct. If this heightens the outrage or forcefulness, go out altogether. That outrage and hatred are left unchecked, they can go to progressively hurtful practices. Request guiding so the manipulator can see unmistakably what they are doing and how to change their practices.

They Search Out the Sensitive, Insecure, or Excessively Trusting

Emotional manipulators search out the vulnerabilities in individuals to misuse them. They may deliberately or unknowingly make relationships with individuals who are the most defenseless and ready to be controlled.

Manipulators can, without much of a stretch, recognize the individuals who have a need to please or who's instabilities drive them to put their own needs behind others' necessities. They may initially appear to be minding and sensitive, utilizing these strategies to redirect their actual thought processes.

Chapter 10:
Psychological Violence of
Narcissistic Abuse

P sychological violence is a form of abuse where the victim is exposed to psychological trauma. Psychological violence happens each time the victim is subjected to emotional distress. In many cases, psychological violence is accompanied by verbal or physical violence.

Many people are victims of psychological violence at some point in time, but they are never aware of it. Without a proper understanding of yourself and your life, you might never know when you are under attack. It also becomes challenging to develop effective strategies you can use to cope with the trauma from such abuse.

In a relationship with a narcissistic partner, several symptoms, reactions, and conditions that the victim might experience are a sign of abuse. The narcissist conditions the victim by creating experiences in relationships that harm the victim.

Relationships

Narcissism has a damaging effect on relationships. Relationships require effort from both partners. As a victim, your relationship is anything but a joint effort. A narcissist partner will turn your life upside down, and by the time they are done with you, you might not have the slightest idea who or what you are.

Intense Insecurities

Your abuser identifies your insecurities and, over time, uses them to put you down. Your insecurities grow stronger, and you cannot trust anyone.

Disbelief in Yourself

Many victims' lives change for the worse because they no longer believe in themselves. Your confidence is eroded to a point where you can no longer trust your judgment.

Anxiety

You live a life of uncertainty and fear. You are always afraid something bad will happen. You don't trust good things because you believe happiness is short-lived and will soon become the worst. You also feel emotionally drained and incapable of enjoying true happiness.

Indecision

Victims who were once grounded become indecisive, confused, and unable to trust anyone, not even themselves.

Esteem Issues

Psychological abuse erodes your confidence. You cannot see yourself as anything better than what your abuser says you are. You shy away from the public, afraid that everyone sees the weaknesses in you.

Rationalizing the Abuse

Abuse in a relationship hurts on so many levels. Victims of narcissists usually end up normalizing the violence to the point where they deny it is happening in the first place. You minimize and rationalize the problem. You will feel your abuser is not a bad person. They had to react the way they did because you probably did something terrible to provoke them.

Fear of Success

Narcissists do not just take away your happiness, they also take away your life. At some point, you stop doing the things you used to love. Success becomes a myth for you because it makes you happy, yet your partner hates it when you derive happiness from others. Talent, happiness, joy, and everything else that interests you become a source of darkness, reprimand, and reprisal.

Self-Destruction and Sabotage

A victim of narcissistic abuse will replay the words and actions in their minds until it becomes second nature. You learn to associate specific actions in the relationship with violence and reprimand. You almost expect a negative reaction from your partner each time you do something. This amplification of negativity will grow into self-sabotage, and if your partner is a malignant narcissist, suicide might not be so far off.

Unhealthy Comparisons

Triangulation is one of the tactics narcissists use to manipulate their victims into submission. It gets worse in a relationship because you end up comparing yourself to someone else all the time. When your partner keeps making you feel you are not good enough and goes as far as introducing a third party into your relationship, it's emotional terrorism. You must fight for their approval and attention to someone else.

Survival through Dissociation

Detachment is a survival technique that many victims of narcissistic abuse embrace. Other than detaching from their partner emotionally, they end up disconnecting from the environment around them. You go through life like a zombie, unable to feel anything. Your life is a mess, and you are unable to connect your emotions to physical sensations. They each exist independently of one another.

Fear of the Unknown

People who have experienced trauma tend to shy away from anything that might relate to it, or symptoms of the traumatic event. It might be a person, a town, a building, and so forth. If something reminds you of the traumatic experience, you are conditioned to avoid it altogether. The same applies to victims of narcissistic abuse.

You find yourself anxious all the time, worried that you might provoke your partner into a fit of rage. You worry about setting boundaries because your partner never seems to recognize them anyway. You want to avoid confronting your partner, and you do your best not to, but they provoke you to get them worked up for some reason.

Unhealthy Compromises

To meet your narcissistic partner's needs, you must compromise on your needs, emotional or otherwise. Everything about you comes second after your partner. Your physical safety also becomes less of a priority to your partner or yourself.

Children and Families

Trust Issues

Life is one big frightening place for a child raised by narcissists. Strings are attached to everything, especially love. Children need unconditional love. However, children of narcissistic parents learn that there is always something attached to it. Toxic people are an embodiment of the same challenges the children endured when growing up. Because their minds have been conditioned to embrace such instances, they are not afraid to interact with toxic people. They learn not to trust or trust too much—this is easier because they have done it all their life.

Inability to Commit

Children raised in a narcissistic environment struggle with commitment issues. When you meet them, they seem like they are looking to establish commitment with someone at first glance. However, deep down, they fear commitment. These kids grow up alienated by the people closest to them, so it is difficult to commit to someone or something. Commitment for such children is often based on what feels right now, not because they want to commit.

Hyperactive Attunement

Hyperactivity is one of the symptoms victims of abuse learn to help them cope with their abuser. It helps them know when things are about to get messy. They are keen on subtle changes in the way the abuser responds to them. This makes them realize changes in facial expression, tone, and so forth. They can also identify the contradiction between gestures and spoken words.

This defense mechanism helps them get through a lot and protects them from the unknown. However, it also breeds a sense of prediction, which can be very unsettling for someone genuine, but does not know how to align their words and gestures. It might be impossible for the child to control how people react, but they can use this technique to choose the relationships they can cultivate or end.

Afraid of Intimacy

Intimacy is an emotional minefield for children raised by narcissists. When they try to open, it is easier to share too much about their struggles hoping that someone might feel their pain and genuinely ease their pain. The challenge here is that they often end up with toxic narcissists whose only desire is to prey on their weaknesses and exploit them for everything they have.

This is one of the reasons why such children are afraid of intimacy in life. Intimacy requires that you open to your partner. You must be vulnerable around one another. You must allow your partner to see you for who you are, with all your weaknesses, embrace you, and love you endlessly.

Affinity for Toxic Relationships

Toxic relationships are typical for children raised by narcissists. They have a lot of experience in this, and it is easier to embrace these relationships because they almost always know what to expect. They embrace abuse as a normal thing, so they find it easier to entertain people who belittle or envy them.

In early adulthood in life, when they take stock of their friendships and relationships, they realize they have so many toxic people in their lives that they are comfortable. This happens because they share a bond. The struggle is all too familiar, and it is the only thing they know.

Emotional Sabotage

Narcissistic parents create an unhealthy relationship with their children. Children grow up afraid. They know one thing leads to another and are pessimistic about some situations. Respect and true love are foreign to them. If they come across someone who loves them unconditionally, it can be unsettling.

Narcissism among Friends

We need friends to help us get through life. We make friends at different stages in life too. Some friends stay with us all our lives, and others fall off along the way. Like any other institution in your life, you need to realize when your friend is a narcissist who will take away everything you hold dear. Energy drain

Think about how long you have been friends. Remember how amazing it used to be to hang out, do all kinds of silly things, or perhaps just enjoy each other's company? Suddenly, you dread hanging out with your friend because you are so drained by the time you leave for your place.

My Way or the Highway

Friendship, like any other relationship, brings two or more people together. You share ideas, experiences, and so much more. A narcissistic friend will always insist that their way is the best. They will be quick to advise you, and failure to follow their advice often results in contempt. Do not be fooled into thinking they are out to help you. This is a manipulative tactic.

Extreme Generosity

There is nothing wrong with kindness. Friends can always volunteer to help one another from time to time. The difference between a genuine friend and a narcissist is that the narcissist will not stop talking about how they help you. They will tell this to anyone who cares to listen. You are nothing but a roadside puppy they picked up in dire need of help.

Unhealthy Trash-Talking

Each level of friendship has its own rules of loyalty and trust. A narcissistic friend is only loyal to themselves. They expect a lot from you in terms of the trust but will stop at nothing to speak ill of your mutual friends. They share stories about your mutual friends that they have no reason to. It is also easier for such friends to frown upon your other friends' successes and even revel in their misfortunes.

Chapter 11:
Dealing with a Narcissist

D ealing with a narcissist is incredibly difficult in the best of times, but there are many ways to manage your relationship. Regardless of whether you are interested in severing all ties for good or are in a position to have to continue some degree of contact with a narcissist, understanding some of the ways to deal with the narcissist's toxic behaviors can help you minimize your risks of harm and abuse. You can also cause the narcissist to lose interest in you and move on to other targets when you prove yourself invulnerable to his manipulative tactics.

Keep in mind that this will be a trial and error effort, and not every method here may be useful or productive in your unique situation. Consider each method carefully to decide if it meets your needs and can help you, and once you have chosen a way, it is essential to remember to keep it up. No matter how much the narcissist may push and try to get your attention back, be consistent to get the best effect from your actions. None of these methods are easy, and each will take a huge amount of effort, but when you finally make it to the other side and realize how very free you are from the narcissist's abuse, you will recognize that it was worth every ounce of effort you put into it.

Cutting off the Narcissist

The easiest way to avoid harm from a narcissist is to end the relationship entirely. Refuse to engage in the relationship at all costs. Taking a huge step back from the relationship may be necessary to clear your head and see things for what they are. This is typically a permanent change and decision and is the only surefire way to make sure that the narcissistic abuse stops. If you refuse to play the game at all, the narcissist cannot manipulate you.

Furthermore, by refusing any engagement or communication with the narcissist, you can deny the narcissist's strongest motivator: Your attention. You suddenly remove yourself as a reliable source of narcissistic supply, and if you continue to deny the narcissist, he will ultimately have to go elsewhere to meet his need.

Remember, the period of leaving an abusive relationship is the most dangerous, and the narcissist likely will rely on every physical and emotional threat he can think of. He may threaten to kill himself, you, or other people, or he may begin stalking you. No matter what he does, refuse to engage, and report erratic or dangerous behavior to the appropriate authorities.

Take a Break from the Relationship

Like cutting off the narcissist, taking a break from the relationship involves a refusal to communicate. In this case, however, it is not permanent. The break is intended to clear your head and reevaluate whether you want to continue the relationship. Regardless of what he may accuse you of, remind yourself that this is not a punishment. You did not make this decision to hurt him; you made it protect and care for yourself. You are entitled to controlling who you communicate with, and if you decide that you do not want to talk to the narcissist, you are within your rights to make that choice.

When taking a break from the narcissist, it is appropriate to tell him once that you are taking a break, and you will discuss things with him when you are ready. You do not have to provide him with a timeline, no matter how much he may pester you for one, and at that point, you refuse all future contact. You are giving yourself the chance to cool off. You are ensuring that you do not say something that will make the situation worse or inflame the narcissist into doing something harmful.

Healthy Boundaries

Sometimes, cutting off a narcissist is not a viable option, and that is okay. When you have no choice but to continue contact, such as if you are bound by court order to maintain a co-parenting relationship, or you work with the narcissist and are not in a position to leave your job, you can focus on mitigating as much harm as possible and protecting yourself from the toxicity the narcissist seems to exude naturally.

Healthy boundaries are among the easiest techniques to minimize harm from a narcissist, but they are difficult. These boundaries represent a line between acceptable and unacceptable to you, and they are to be set at your prerogative. Limitations are a healthy part of every relationship, regardless of whether it is a marriage, a friendship, or even with your children. Without limits, you will find yourself continually stepping on toes and breeding resentment.

Narcissists see boundaries as the ultimate insult. It is irresistible to the narcissist, and he will try to stomp on them at every turn. The limitations set are nothing more than challenges; games to get rises out of you and exert control over your emotional state. When you set these boundaries, you must be prepared to enforce and defend them at all costs.

Disengage

When cutting off is not an option, the next best thing is disengaging emotionally. If you do not invest any emotional energy into your interactions with the narcissist, he will eventually lose interest in you. You can keep your interactions relatively unchanged, but do not pay any attention to the words said, no matter how hurtful they may be.

Try to keep in mind that people with NPD are stuck in a developmental stage of a child, unable to feel empathy and wired to be selfish, and remind yourself that if a child had said the things the narcissist spewed at you, you would likely not be very upset or offended at all. After all, children are impulsive, emotional, and irrational. The narcissist hits all three of those traits on the nose, and you should not take the narcissist's actions personally at all.

Disengaging does not mean ignoring or bottling your feelings, however. When you disconnect, acknowledge what was said and give it the consideration it deserves, which is, admittedly, very little. This can particularly difficult if the narcissist is a loved one that you trusted but remember to try to disregard the emotional reactions to the words that protect you. You do not fall into the narcissist's trap, and you do not let the narcissist regain control over your emotions, and in return, the narcissist will slowly lose interest.

The Grey Rock Method

Like disengaging emotionally, this method involves minimizing emotional reactions, but in this case, it is ignoring all interactions, both good and bad. You aim to avoid as much interaction as possible, and when you are forced to interact, you should keep it boring and meaningless.

If you can achieve this state of mediocrity, the narcissist will slowly lose interest in you. The trick in interacting is to tell you to be robotic in responses. No matter how angry you may feel in response to whatever was said, respond in as few words as possible, and make sure it is never immediately after the message was sent if it does not warrant an immediate response.

Be Realistic

Keeping your interactions with the narcissist realistic will keep you from setting up high standards that she will never meet. Telling yourself that she will never be emotionally supportive of you and that it is a personality limit that she lacks empathy will help you keep reality in mind when dealing with a narcissist. If you are fully prepared for the narcissist to respond in typical narcissist fashion, you will always be prepared, no matter how she responds, and you may even find that you are surprised on occasion. This is key when you are maintaining a relationship with a narcissist, whether romantic, platonic, workplace, familial, or co-parenting. You are protected from the disappointment of narcissistic behavior.

Keep in mind that being realistic does not excuse abuse. It is never okay for someone to hurt you or step on your boundaries. However, if you know that narcissists do those, you will not be as blindsided when it does happen, and you can better prepare in advance to protect yourself. You should still correct negative or unproductive behaviors, even if it is unpleasant or you would rather avoid doing so.

Decide Your Hill to Die on

The last important tactic to remember is to choose your hill to die on wisely. This is a fancy way of saying choose your battles carefully. Though narcissists seek out confrontation-avoidant people on purpose, preferring to avoid conflict can be a way to prevent detection too. Thus, you should always pick your battles wisely and only be prepared to engage in a conflict if you genuinely want to deal with the aftermath.

While some things are worthy of a conflict, such as a co-parent choosing to drive with children in the car while drunk, an argument over who said something first is petty, and the narcissist is unlikely to concede or admit that he is lying. For this reason, you should only choose battles if you are willing to fight for them. If you are unwilling to deal with the aftermath and ultimately, whatever the narcissist did is insignificant, do not bother fighting over it.

Chapter 12:
Stopping Abuse

Now that you understand what narcissism is and what narcissistic abuse looks like, you are ready to think about how you can fight back. Many men and women involved in relationships with narcissists do not see fighting back as an important step. They may be happy, good-natured people who want to get along with everyone.

Fighting back will involve learning how to protect yourself from the narcissist in your life. The best first defense against the narcissist is understanding that the narcissist is a manipulator.

They manipulate naturally, just as the pathological liar lies naturally and spontaneously. Understanding this about the narcissist will help you approach every interaction with them from the standpoint of vulnerability.

We will explore some strategies and things you can keep in mind to help arm you against the narcissist. This is a useful way of thinking about this process: girding yourself in armor against the narcissist's attacks.

Tip #1. Be Conscious of the Personal, Delicate Details You Give the Narcissist

This may be a hard pill for some to swallow, but the narcissist can manipulate and control you because you have given them the information they need. You have told them, without words, what makes you sad, angry, or happy. They have observed your gestures to know when you like a new person, or you dislike them. They even know when you are interested in sex and disinterested.

The narcissist has been observing you from the very beginning, and you have allowed them to make a working list of all the personal details about yourself. Although it is not always easy to be reserved if you are naturally an outgoing, friendly person, holding your cards a little closer to your chest can go a long way. Be careful of what you say to the narcissist and conscious of those gestures that give valuable information away.

Tip #2. Do Not Allow the Narcissist to Touch You during Conversation

This is a tip that comes straight from the Neurolinguistic Programming handbook. Practitioners of this art learn various tools of ingratiating themselves with others. It is about getting other people to like you.

The narcissist, too, wants you to like him or her because that will make it all the easier for them to manipulate you. One simple way that narcissists ingratiate themselves with their targets is by touching them (a hand or a leg) during a conversation. Do not allow the narcissist to touch you because it is a trick to turn you into a hapless victim.

Tip #3. Be Conscious of Gestures the Narcissist Uses to Ingratiate Themselves with You, like Mimicking Your Movements

The narcissist has several weapons at hand when it comes to getting an "in" with their target. We have spoken of how they may touch you to cause you to feel positively towards them, but they also can mimic your gestures or even your words. This strategy is well-known in NLP, but little known elsewhere.

It is natural for people to seek closeness with others and to be part of a group. Very suggestible people can even become victims to people who have subtly mimicked their movements (like how they push their hair behind their ears or the way they turn their heads to the side when they laugh). If you are having dinner with the narcissist, they may order the same meal you ordered. It seems silly, but it is effective at establishing closeness with others. Be suspicious of the little tricks that they will use to inspire a false sense of closeness and rapport.

Tip #4. Be Wary of a Disconnect Between the Narcissist's Facial Expression or Demeanor and What They Are Saying

The narcissist is, at the core, a false person. The narcissist may be false because they recognize that they must be this way to manipulate people or be insincere for other reasons. But the narcissist will give you clues to what they think and feel if you are paying attention. Because the narcissist behaves falsely, there will often be disconnected between what they say and what their facial expressions tell you. They may say they love you, but their eyes are cold and distant. They may express sympathy at your tragedies, but their eyes and lips are smiling. Learn to notice these subtle clues that the narcissist is not who they appear to be. This will help you realize that the narcissist is not as dear to you as you perhaps thought previously.

Tip #5. Be Sensitive to When You Feel Emotional or Uneasy During a Conversation for No Reason

Sometimes the first clue that something is not right is just that: not feeling right. If you find that you were happy before a conversation with this person and now you are said or were thinking before, and now you are confused, this may be a sign that the narcissist is manipulating you in ways too subtle for you to detect. Learn to be intuitive about these things. Perhaps the thing you agreed to do in the conversation you should revisit.

Your goal in dealing with the narcissist is to be prepared to protect yourself. Before now, you were the unfortunate tool of the narcissist who used you in ways that you had not noticed before. You did not know that they were making you sad and self-conscious to isolate and control you. You did not know that they were using subtle strategies to establish false closeness and rapport with you. What you need to understand to act against the narcissist, that is, to protect yourself from further abuse, is that you do not have a close relationship with the narcissist.

The narcissist often does not feel close to anyone. They have a world view which places them at the center, and they see others as tools to accomplish their end. Once you begin to doubt the narcissist's motivations, as you naturally will, you will learn that it is in your best interest to establish some distance; some boundaries, if you will. This often happens as you gain more awareness of the nature of the narcissist and your relationship.

Chapter 13:
Make Sure You Set Boundaries

When you walk out of a narcissistic relationship, it is essential to build a shield around yourself, and one of the ways to achieve this is to put some physical distance between yourself and your ex. You should also checkmate the things that remind you of your ex, because such memories will only trigger your pain, and potentially slow down your recovery. To achieve this, you are advised to avoid stalking them, and rather blacklist their emails, social media handles, and phone numbers.

Another effective way of building a boundary around you is by mastering the art of saying no. It is essential to say no to certain propositions, especially when they lack substance or any real value. The habit of saying 'No' will help you build self-respect and real confidence.

Get Rid of the Toxicity

When victims of narcissistic relationships look back at the time they spent with their partners and consider how they did everything within their power to please and appease them, they realize how painful the process has been. The amount of time they've wasted.

The truth is that these people have been exposed to some severe mental disorder, which is generally unhealthy for their mental wellbeing.

When empaths go into relationships with narcissists, they make major sacrifices to keep their partners happy, and most times, they go as far as putting their partner's interests first. Sadly, these self-serving and manipulative narcissistic individuals know all about this. Rather than appreciate it, they take full advantage—their manipulative ways only result in pain and anguish in their partner's lives, and to a lot of toxicity. However, now that the relationship is over, it is time to get rid of the toxicity by restoring some level of clarity, and the way to go about it is to externalize it.

When you externalize, you'll realize that your chaotic thoughts begin to form meaningful patterns bit by bit. There are several other forms of externalization methods, including yoga, dance, massage, sweating, deep breathing, etc. When you indulge in these practices, your body will naturally metabolize the toxic chemicals that have been generated during the different stages of the failed relationship.

Embrace the Truth and Forgive Yourself

This is a very critical step because it helps in setting your mind straight. During this stage, you will have to embrace the truth by accepting that your ex was not only toxic but was also out to hurt you knowingly. Realize you have been manipulated, abused, and tricked! Your high threshold for pain worked in your abuser's advantage, and he kept pushing you farther and farther with each round of abuse.

The fact that you genuinely loved your partner made it difficult for you to see the warning signs, and your best traits were explored and used against you: openness, desire to explore, empathy and positivity, etc. When you accept the truth, you'll realize that none of it was your fault. Thus, you'll have to forgive yourself.

Accept the Fact That Part of You Knew

You must accept the fact that a part of you knew, but you choose to ignore it. This is an essential step because it involves taking responsibility (do not confuse it with self-blame) and carrying out a post-mortem analysis of all that happened during the relationship.

You must have ignored some weird feelings you had during the early stages of the relationship. Maybe a couple of things he said didn't add up. Go back in your mind and ask yourself why you chose to disregard your basic instincts.

It is usual for people that weren't loved by their parents as kids to seek fulfillment elsewhere in their adult lives, and it is a serious vulnerability. Especially in the hands of these narcissistic predators who can easily detect that urge for love and be attracted to it, just like the scent of fresh blood attracts sharks.

In this world, your instinct is your best friend, and the more you listen to it, the more embolden it becomes. It may be hard for you to connect with your instincts after such an abusive relationship, and the reason is that people become hypersensitive due to PTSD.

Embark on a Soul Search

The process of surviving and healing from an abusive relationship presents a wonderful opportunity for you to learn and grow. The reason is that you'll see all your vulnerabilities. When you ascertain your weaknesses, you'll know precisely how to go about fixing issues. However, many people lack this knowledge, and that's why most of them are stuck with the same style for most of their lives, even while seeking change.

Real change emanates from deep work, and the key to this process is soul searching (or self-inquiry). When you walk out of an abusive narcissistic relationship, you might be physically free, but a part of you is still stuck in a mental prison, and the only way to be truly free is to reawaken your mind through soul searching.

When you do some proper soul searching, you might realize that some of the vulnerabilities that attract manipulators into your life include;

- Your desire for security – Sometimes, when their fathers neglect children during childhood, it comes back to haunt them in the future. A father figure is important in a child's life because one of his fundamental responsibilities is to instill a sense of self-protection in his children. When children lack this essential element, they grow into adults with an impaired sense of security.

- Your desire for adoration – When insensitive and ignorant parents raise children, they mostly grow into adults who display symptoms of a total lack of confidence and low self-esteem. Thus, making them extremely vulnerable to narcissistic predators, that only need to shower them with praises in other to achieve their aims.

- Your desire for acknowledgment – Many people lack self-confidence, which makes them seek validation and acceptance unknowingly. Sometimes, even people that have accomplished a lot in life still have these traits, because lack of confidence doesn't dwell on the surface, it is rooted somewhere in their subconscious. Thus, to have a go at it, you must master the art of self-talk, which will ultimately lead you to self-dependence (the greatest key to freedom).

Chapter 14:
Effects of Narcissistic Abuse over Time

Once the narcissist can get ahold of you, it will not take long before they start to do as much damage as possible. And because of their tactics, the abuse from this person is likely going to continue for several years, if not longer. This is never something that lasts a few weeks, or a few months only and then is done with for good. The narcissist is not going to give up without a fight. And since the victim often doesn't understand what is going on around them, they will usually stay in this kind of abusive relationship for a long time, and deal with the consequences in the process.

It is essential to recognize some of the signs and symptoms that can come into play when a narcissist abuses someone for any amount of time, but mainly what happens when this person is under the control of their narcissistic partner or parent, or even someone else in their lives, for a long period. The changes that happen to a person are going to be outstanding and learning how to recognize the signs and avoid them as much as possible can be critical.

When we think about abuse in most cases, we often think about physical abuse first. But there are different forms of violence that we may have to deal with, and emotional abuse is one of the worst.

We need to look at the signs of a narcissist taking over. These signs are pretty much going to be part of the effects that happen with narcissistic abuse over time, especially when the victim does not recognize what is going on. Emotional abuse is going to be about as dangerous as physical abuse, and often it is going to come before it. Sometimes, these two types of abuse are going to happen together.

The first thing to realize is that if you have been abused emotionally, it is not your fault. There is also not a correct way that you are meant to feel about this situation. Emotional abuse is not going to be normal, but the feelings you have in this situation are normal.

In the beginning, you may notice that there is some denial that you feel at first. It is hard for most people to realize that they are dealing with a narcissist and are in this kind of situation to start with. Often, we won't believe it, and it is entirely natural to hope that you are a bit wrong with this. You may have some feelings of shame, hopelessness, fear, and confusion.

This is not where it all is going to end, though. Even if it just happens on occasion or for the short term with the narcissist, this emotional toll can come with some other side effects, including physical and behavior.

You may experience some issues, including:

- Aches and pains in different parts of the body that you can't explain.

- Racing heartbeat.

- Nightmares that won't go away.

- Muscle tension from tensing up the body during any interactions with the narcissist.

- Lots of moodiness, because you can't express your feelings and are anxious about what is going to happen next.

- A lot of trouble concentrating because you are focusing on what the narcissist is talking about.

When the abuse goes on for a longer period, there will be some other side effects as well. Studies have shown that severe emotional abuse, including what we see in a narcissistic relationship, can be as powerful as physical abuse. Of course, if this goes on for a longer period, both will lead us to feel depression and low self-esteem. You may also develop issues including:

- Social withdrawal (which is going to be something that the narcissist tries to manufacture), and loneliness

- Insomnia

- Guilt all the time

- Chronic pain that you are not able to explain away.

- Lots of anxiety

The longer the abuse from the narcissist goes on, the worse the symptoms will get. And this is how the target gets stuck in a loop that is so bad for them. The target feels low self-esteem, deals with a lot of different health conditions, and starts to rely entirely on the narcissist. This will ensure that the narcissist can get what they want, but leaves the target feeling lost and confused, without the right way to deal with the issues.

Some researchers theorize that this emotional abuse could contribute to the development of other conditions, including post-traumatic stress disorder, fibromyalgia, and chronic fatigue syndrome.

Chapter 15:
Co-parenting with a Narcissist

W hat if you end a relationship with a narcissist, but you have children together? This complicates the situation, but don't be hopeless. Your child can still grow up healthy and happy; you will have to be the responsible, consistent figure in their lives. Unfortunately, you cannot depend on your ex to pull their weight in this way. This explores what your child might be going through, prioritizes their well-being, and how-to co-parent with an ex who will never cooperate the way you want. This will seem overwhelming—how can you embody the role of two parents while combating your ex's toxicity?—so you will also learn some self-care methods.

You know what it's like to be the partner of a narcissist, but what about a child? It's important to understand what your kid is going through if their other parent—your ex—is a narcissist. Depending on how long you were with your ex with a child or children in the mix, you've probably noticed the unhealthy aspects of their parenting style. Here are some common consequences:

The Child's Needs and Wants Are Ignored

Like their partner, a narcissist won't pay attention to what their child needs or wants. The narcissist's needs always take priority, so the child learns from a young age that what they want doesn't matter. They are never nurtured and taught to feel safe. They feel small and insignificant. These kids may not even know how to express what they want and need because that type of thinking has never been encouraged. Their sense of self can be very stunted.

To counter this messaging, encourage your child to pursue their dreams, and show interest in what they're into. Know how they feel and what they think about things, whether it's movies, friendships, or the separation from your ex. If your kid expresses a lot of insecurity and self-doubt, gently guide them, so they feel like they have support and freedom. This guidance can be applied to finding a hobby or having conversations about their feelings about their life.

The Child Has A Lot of Anxiety About Their Worth

Narcissists frequently put very high expectations on their kids. They believe their kids reflect on them, so they push them to succeed. The child won't feel loved unless they're doing something well, looking a certain way, or thinking certain things. The narcissist might be very critical, judgmental, and withholding when their kid inevitably "fails." The child will feel like nothing they do is ever good enough. It's very common for these kids to have low self-esteem and poor self-worth because they believe love is conditional.

Pushing back against the belief that love is conditional is arguably the most important thing you can do as a parent. Parents should always be the people a child can rely on for love, no matter what. If your ex isn't capable of being that, it's more important that you take on that role wholeheartedly. Always celebrate your child, especially when they "fail" or don't meet the expectations your ex set up. Let them know your love isn't dependent on their successes; you love them because of who they are, not what they do. You can still encourage them to improve and set goals, but never attach your attention and affection to an outcome. Be sure to tell them you love them no matter what, too. Words are powerful.

The Child Is the One Taking Care of Their Parent's Emotional Needs

From a very young age, the children of narcissists learn to always tiptoe around their parents. They figure out quickly that their parent's emotions are unstable and prone to quick change. The parent will start looking to the child to help them work through things. This can result in telling them things that are too mature for the child to deal with and expecting support. The child becomes the responsible one—the voice of reason—way too soon. Their own emotions are neglected, and the child can't develop healthy self-care skills.

What can you do to help your child learn to take care of themselves and not worry about you? Model good self-care. When you get upset, don't lose control around your kid. That includes any strong emotions, like grief or anger. However, you should encourage your kid to express those emotions when they need to. Be a safe place, a shoulder to cry on. When they get angry, help them figure out healthy ways of expression instead of punishing them. They'll see that you are emotionally stable and nurturing, even when their other parent can't be.

Recovery from a relationship with a narcissist is complicated if you have kids. Odds are you won't be able to stick to a non-contact rule or cut them out of your life completely. Hopefully, you can if there was abuse in the relationship, and the law protects you, but even then, things don't always go the way they should. If your ex wants to be involved in your children's lives, there are certain things you can do to make the process easier and safer.

Set Communication Limitations

As a co-parent, you will need to talk to your ex. However, you can decide when you talk and about what. Your ex will always try to push the boundaries and use any opportunity to get under your skin. They may even try to get you so angry that you lose control, which gives them leverage. Avoid talking on the phone or in-person if your ex likes to go on rants, emotionally abuse you, or try to get you worked up. Stick to emails, which gives you more control over what you say, and it keeps everything in writing.

It's impossible to control what your ex says when your kid is with them. However, when the kid is with you, you can set more boundaries. Expect your ex to want to talk to the kid a lot. Set a schedule and stick to it.

Protect Your Child

It's hard to control what your ex says if your ex has custody or visitation rights. However, you should never use your child as a messenger pigeon. Don't ask them to communicate with your ex on your behalf or ask them to spy. This puts the kid in a very awkward and possibly scary situation. You can find out how they're being treated and what they're doing by having normal conversations. If you're concerned by something they say, ask them a question like, "How does that make you feel?" It can be hard to know what to say, and there are certain things your child might not want to talk about with you, so getting your kid to counseling is an excellent idea.

You will feel a lot of emotions, especially negative ones, during a co-parenting scenario with a narcissist. Don't use your child as a sounding board for your frustrations with your ex. This not only makes the kid feel like they need to comfort you and manage your feelings; it makes them feel torn about their love for their other parent. They might instinctively resist your criticisms and jump to your ex's defense or become angry and even scared of their other parent.

The More Written Detail, the Better

Co-parenting with a narcissist is complicated, and every situation is a little different. One of the best things anyone can do is keep detailed records. Right at the beginning, when you start seeing a family law attorney, tell them what's going on with your ex. Tell them they are a narcissist and are "high-conflict," a legal term for these types of custody scenarios. In your custody agreement, write down every detail, like who pays for the days and times they have visitation, holiday visitations, and more.

Having detailed records is also important as life continues because your ex is unlikely to follow the rules peacefully. They will try to push back and having records of their bad behavior protects you and your child(ren). If they cancel or try to move around visitation, write it down. If they refuse to pay for something or are late with the money, write it down. Are they using phone calls to manipulate your kid? Inform them that you are going to be recording the call. Any communication between you two should be saved, if possible. This evidence lets you hold them accountable.

What You Can Do to Be a Better Parent

By now, you know that your ex will never be a good co-parent. Parenting is all about putting your child's needs before your own, and narcissists can do that with anyone. At least, not consistently. This means you must be both a parent and someone who counters any toxic, negative messaging coming from your ex. You'll feel overwhelmed. How can you accomplish this?

Take Care of Yourself

Self-care is not selfish. As a parent, this has never been truer. If you let yourself get drained, worn down, and depleted, you'll have nothing to offer your kid. You'll have less patience, less stability, and more irritability. Your kid won't come to you because they'll see how exhausted you are, and they won't want to burden you. Not only will you not have the physical or emotional energy to care for them, but you're modeling unhealthy habits they will imitate. They won't know how to take care of themselves, and like you, they'll burn out. For both your sake and the sake of your kids, practice good self-care.

Find a Community

Your child may essentially lack a second parent, but that doesn't mean you're in this alone. Don't burden yourself by believing you are your kid's only adult role model. Find a community that is supportive of both you and your child and rich with healthy, loving people who can encourage your child's emotional growth. A community can also help you by giving you friends to vent to, who are happy to babysit, and more. People need community, especially when life gets rough. And how important healthy relationships are after you leave a narcissist, and that's even truer if you have a child.

Don't Let Your Ex Manipulate You

One of the best things you can do is not let your ex infect you with toxic thoughts and beliefs to be a good parent. Expect to hear things like, "How could you do this to our family?" They will try to make you guilty for leaving and say that the separation is bad for your children. When they see you aren't budging, they'll move on to the custody agreement, and say, "That's bad, too." Don't believe it. You know what your ex was like. They will be just as critical and selfish in their relationship with their child as they were with you, so leaving and sticking to a certain arrangement is the only healthy thing.

Your ex probably won't stay quiet about their frustrations and trash you on social media and to anyone who will listen. Having people, even friends, believe you are a bad parent can be hard. Keep a standing firm and remember that this is what's best for your child. The people who know you will be supportive.

Chapter 16:
Things to Remember Before Making an Escape Plan

Most domestic abuse victims go through emotional turmoil and are in two minds before deciding to do so. Some facts to consider before you go ahead with your decision are.

Set Realistic Expectations

We all hope that things change magically, but they never do. Expecting the abuser to change or hoping that this is the last time it happens will keep the abuse going. Studies have shown that most abusers continue to misbehave with the victim because they feel that the victims are helpless and need the abusers' support to sustain. The only thing that victims should believe in is that they are self-dependent and are doing the right thing by standing up against the torture.

Know That You Cannot Help Them

Being on drugs or being temporarily intoxicated does not justify the abuser's behavior. Treating someone else with violence is a heinous act regardless of circumstance. It is natural for victims to try to help the abuser if they are in a close relationship, but in most instances, they make it worse for themselves. It is better to accept that you are living with an abuser, seek professional or legal help if you can, and move on before it is too late.

Promises Are Meant to Be Broken

There may be hundreds of promises that the abuser makes each time after he commits a mistake. They may plead for a last chance, cry for help, play the victim, or hurt themselves to prove their love. In any case, victims should keep a firm grip on their rational thinking and differentiate between the possible and impossible. Fake promises and pathological lying habits are traits that many abusers have in common.

Don't Worry About What Happens After You Leave

"Will he be able to manage his food without me?" "Who will pack his bags when I am not around?" "Can our kids cope with the stress of their parents separating?"

Unfortunately, the scenario worsens when there is a child involved in the abuse. It is okay for victims to worry about the aftermath of their decision, but at the same time, ensuring safety for themselves and their kids, is also equally important.

You Are Not Needy

If you talk to your friends about your situation or ask for help from your family, it does not mean that you are emotionally weak. Self-expression is a personal strength that helps victims of violence to move on and start again. It is common for abusers to make you feel vulnerable, but you must continue believing in yourself and progress with confidence. Remember that it is okay to make mistakes or ask for help; being harsh on yourself is not on the cards.

Be Prepared to Leave at Any Moment

If you have been in an abusive relationship for over one year, then there will be chances that the violence will increase with time. Be mentally prepared to leave the house at any point you feel your life is in danger. Always keep your car fueled and have the keys close to you so that you can grab them in case of an emergency. Keep the emergency bag as detailed above, ready.

Practice Escaping

Practicing your escape can prevent victims from getting confused at the heat of the moment. Rehearse in your mind about how you can escape when the fight gets ugly or who to call if you are hurt. If you have kids, plan, and rehearse for their escape as well.

Have a Backup Plan

Escaping from an abuser who is close to us can be tricky since he is already aware of our whereabouts and contacts. Keep a secret confidante, for example, a colleague that the abuser may not know, a relative, a neighbor, or an old friend. Inform them about your situation and let them know where you might seek refuge if you must leave the house in a panic.

Do Not Compromise

If you have decided to leave the abuser and choose a peaceful life for yourself, there is no probably little reason to rethink it. Being self-compassionate is an essential requisite to heal your wounds. The perpetrator may invariably try to make you feel that it's your fault and portray themselves as the victims. Keep the authorities informed; a crucial aspect of the safety plan is to have a reliable support system. Thankfully, a robust legal team supports men and women of all ages facing abuse at home or outside. If you feel unsafe being around a person, no matter how close he/she is to you, inform the police or a community support worker about it.

Even after leaving an abusive relationship, the abuser may continue stalking the victim, sending messages, calling at vulnerable times of the day, or showing up everywhere. Victims need to have a firm grip of themselves under such circumstances and, if possible, stay in a group to ensure safety.

Seeking professional assistance to overcome the trauma is entirely acceptable and often necessary to help victims move on with their lives. Individual therapy, group counseling, peer mental health programs, trauma interventions, and resilience training are some ways you could train yourself to recover from emotional distress.

In a toxic relationship, the victims often lose their identity and sense of self. If the victim is a child or a young adult, they might grow up to become indecisive, underconfident, and always look for someone to control their lives. Studies have shown that children who have been abused in their early years are more likely to get involved in abusive relationships in the future as well.

The control and dominance that accompanies a violent relationship take a toll on the victim's mental health, ultimately making him apathetic and doubtful about themselves. Leaving a toxic relationship with a broken heart and an anxious mind is not easy. It takes a lot of courage and self-motivation to take a step forward and say 'no' to someone close to you. Finding the strength to walk out takes time and support, and here are some self-help strategies for victims that can help them execute their plan efficaciously.

Reflect on Yourself

Know yourself before you plan to move out. Studies have proved that abusers have a strong understanding of the victim's mind. He is aware of how the victims think and use the knowledge to manipulate them emotionally.

The root of feeling trapped may lie inside the victim. So, before you move out, spend some time knowing your mind. Talk to a therapist, write thought journals, chat with your friends, practice mindfulness, and have a moment with yourself as often as you can. The clearer you get about your thought patterns and emotional experiences, the easier it will be to successfully live an independent life.

Emotional Distancing

Abuse coming from families is the hardest one to get rid of. Nine times out of ten, families are imposed on us; we have no control, and neither do we have the choice to select who we are related to. More than 60% of sexual abuse incidents in childhood are caused by people the children know and are close to—including family members, relatives, schoolteachers, and other staff, servants, and the list goes on.

Abusers, in all forms, are 'emotional vampires.' They establish their authority and suck away all the positive energy. The emotional blundering associated with any misbehavior makes the burden heavier to carry. A good idea to avoid this is emotionally distancing yourself from the abuser. Besides saving victims from being manipulated, emotionally distancing yourself also makes it easy to plan a life without the abuser dominating it.

Self-Determination

Many abusive relationships are built on power games. If the batterer feels powerful and in charge of the victim's life, he feels emotionally satisfied and secure. Psychologists agree that showing confidence, even if you don't necessarily feel that confidence, can help in getting your autonomy back.

You have decided not to tolerate the abuse anymore. You are now determined to start anew and be safe. You know that you deserve better, you know that you deserve to be happy, and what you will seek from now on. You feel more positive, more empowered, more self-motivated, and more confident. You feel ready to take a step forward in life. And you are now ready to clean up the mess that someone else created in your life.

Chapter 17:
Healing from Narcissistic Abuse if Codependent

W hen you end the relationship with the "no contact" method, you will go through a period of pain. Since you were codependent for so long, it will take time to move on emotionally. After enough time passes, you will realize that life goes on without them, and things will start to feel normal again.

There will be a part of you that tries to delude yourself into thinking you don't have to leave them. That is why it is so essential for you to look at the facts. If you keep making yourself aware of the facts, you will know that leaving them is best. It will remind you that you don't need their permission because they won't give it to you. The fact that they have this much control over you is the entire problem.

The very first thing to understand about seeking freedom from a narcissist is to cut off all ties and avoid contact with them all together. The main reason why it is so difficult to let go is because of the emotional attachment. They struggle with the idea that they can help their narcissistic relationship. That's why they stay longer than they should.

One of the things you can do to help yourself continue with a no-contact order is through writing. To be specific, make a 'trauma' journal. Trauma journals are designed to remind you of the abuse you have experienced from the narcissist. Write down what happened, how it made you feel, what you tried to do about it, etc. Write down what you remember and right when it happens.

No-Contact Rule

- NO meeting with the narcissist – in public, private, with friends, or any other circumstance

- NO phone calls – including calling them or answering them on a friend's phone

- NO text messages – including when they try to reach you through someone you know or ask a mutual friend how they are doing

- NO social media messaging – Facebook, Instagram, Bumble, Twitter, Snapchat, WhatsApp, etc.

- NO third-party contact – including any friends, family members, or anyone associated with the narcissist

Make it known to your mutual friends or family members that you are not having any contact with your narcissistic abuser. Create some boundaries and limits for people who continue talking about them. One thing is sure: the no-contact rule is going to be extremely difficult and may take you to an emotional rollercoaster for the first bit of recovery. That is especially true when the narcissist happens to be your mother.

The narcissist may want to lash out at you and make you feel guilty for ending the relationship and permanently getting rid of them. In their failed attempts to reach you (hopefully), they may start trying to be nice. For example, if they have contacted you or still think you are getting their messages, it may start like, "Why are you not talking to me? I thought you loved me." When the guilting, gaslighting, manipulating, and hurtful techniques wear off, they may try saying, "I am truly sorry for everything I have done to you. I miss you, so please come home, and I will do everything to make this right."

Leaving a codependent and narcissistic relationship fills our heads with so many contradictory feelings. We know that we are unhappy, but at the same time, we don't know how to leave. We don't know how to leave because the relationship has filled our entire consciousness for a very long time. Once you can let go of how you suffered because of your ex, you will be ready to start the next phase of your life.

Just like a house that has four walls, you are also made up of four walls. These four walls or pillars make you the person you are and help you create an identity for yourself.

A narcissist's relationship hurts so much and causes internal damage because a narcissist methodically attacks all the four pillars. He ensures that he leaves no stone unturned in damaging every small part of all the four pillars leaving no option other than falling.

The destruction is so much that it takes months and, in some cases, years for the pillars to rebuild.

Here are some practices to help rebuild the pillars:

Self-Esteem

Self-esteem essentially means supporting yourself. It is how much control you have over yourself, your mind, body, and behaviors. Self-esteem is also about the perception you have about yourself and how you see yourself. The opposite of self-esteem is self-sabotage or self-damage. During the process of healing, you must build your self-esteem.

You can begin by doing simple things that tell you that you are in control of the situation. You can start by tackling basic hygiene things that you might be ignoring right now because of your PTSD or depression. Something as simple as having a daily routine to shower or dress decently even when at home can help you regain a sense of control. These baby steps will help you tackle the bigger problems.

Self-Worth

This is about knowing your value and respecting your worth. It believes that you are worth the respect, love, and affection. The exact opposite of self-worth is shame and unworthiness.

After the abuse, the narcissist would have ensured that you feel a deep sense of shame and hate yourself. Self-worth is about speaking up for your rights and standing up for yourself and what you believe in.

You need to focus on the courage to build self-worth. Courage does not mean trying to scale the mountains or running in the wild. Courage means taking measures to change your life actively. It can be applying for another job, negotiating good pay that you deserve, applying to school if you always wanted to finish school, etc. It means identifying something that you wanted to do but have never done because you believed that you were not worth it.

Self-Trust

Self-trust is about trusting yourself, your judgment. It means having faith in yourself and being confident about your decisions. It means not second-guessing every single decision and worrying about it.

When you lack self-trust, you live in constant fear and doubt. During the relationship with the narcissist, you slowly start losing self-trust without even you realize. It happens silently, and before you know it, you will be second-guessing everything. The narcissist achieves this by gaslighting and deflecting blame.

The only way to rebuild self-trust is to listen to your intuition. The gut feeling that everyone talks about is what you must pay attention to. Trust that instinct and let it go. Gut feeling is more tangible than some more forms of intuition. Gut feeling is never wrong, as it is your inner voice trying to guide you and protect you from danger or something that is not right for you.

Your gut feeling and intuition stop working once you start ignoring them. It is like ignoring your best friend who has nothing but the best intentions for you. Once you start ignoring your intuition and gut, they no longer guide you, and that is when you take the wrong steps.

Get it back by listening to it. Follow whatever your gut says and see the change.

Self-Love

Finally, the fourth pillar, self-love, is about caring and nurturing yourself. It is about treating yourself well. Self-love takes a back seat during a narcissist relationship because it wants and demands all the love. When you are in a relationship with a narcissist, you cease to be in a relationship with yourself. You slowly stop loving yourself and go into self-denial and self-judgment mode. You judge yourself poorly and try to rationalize all the bad behavior being shown by the narcissist. When you do not love yourself, you go into a people-pleasing mode and develop a savior complex. By now, you know how dangerous savior complex is to your health and sanity. You start believing you are ugly and stop taking care of your health.

The medicine to this lies in loving yourself back. This can be accomplished by taking small steps such as cooking your favorite meal, eating healthy food, and eating regular meals. It could also be treating yourself at a salon or spa and just pampering yourself.

You can focus on things that you want to change about yourself and, more importantly, accept what you cannot change. Self-acceptance is a part of self-love because if you do not accept yourself just as you are, then there is no way that another person or the world will accept you the way you are. This is because others will treat you just as well or as bad as you treat yourself. By treating yourself well, you teach the world how to treat you and convey your boundaries and wishes to them.

You may go to bed a lot of days, wishing that you do not have to get up the following morning because you are afraid of how bad the day will be. You will constantly feel like there is no light at the end of the tunnel.

Do not drown in this hopelessness because this kind of negative thinking will quickly take you back to victim land. The journey to victim land is a free airplane ride where you will reach the deepest levels of fear, hatred, and disgust within minutes, but remember that victim land journey means no return.

Think that God has given you this amazing opportunity to heal you, and you can start by drawing closer to him. The healing that comes from your spirit is what you need for psychological abuse, just because many of the scars you have are not physical ones.

Healing depends on various factors, but above all, it depends on how committed you are to the process. At times you will see no progress at all. There will also be times when you will take two steps back from one forward stage for reasons you cannot understand yourself.

Chapter 18:
Resisting Reconciliation with the Narcissist

O nce you leave the narcissist, you may feel like a huge weight has lifted from your chest. You feel like you can breathe again for the first time in a long time. You feel like you have made the right choice for yourself. However, you find that the narcissist is back on your doorstep in a short time, knocking at your door and asking you to come back or take him back. If he is not trying to get you to go back to him, you may begin to miss him.

This is only natural and is nothing to be ashamed of— when you have spent a part of your life with someone you have loved, you will miss him naturally. You can miss him without going back, however, and you can truly stay away from when you can recognize that. Remember, staying away is what is in your own best interest. You must be able to stay away from the narcissist to protect yourself. You owe it to yourself to make sure that you stay away and truly heal into the person you know you can be.

It is only natural that you may yearn for that connection, especially the connection that you had at the beginning. However, you must resist it to help yourself. These steps will help you keep yourself busy and reminded that the abuse did happen, and it is because it happened that you cannot afford to go back to the narcissist.

Resist the Temptation to Judge and Blame Yourself

As you begin to heal away from the narcissist, it can become easy to allow the blame to shift back to yourself. When you have nothing but time to yourself to think about what has happened, you may find that you are unhappy with the way things turned out. You may feel guilty, asking yourself how you could let yourself get caught up into a relationship like that in the first place. You may find that you are angry with yourself, wondering how you could not see the red flags when they were right in front of your face. You may feel like you made a royal mistake, and that you should have done better. This can lead to you judging and blaming yourself, which will hurt your self-esteem even more.

This is what the narcissist would want you to do—when feeling like you were to blame, you may question why you would deserve to escape in the first place. You may begin to feel like you do not deserve better, which will lead to your unconscious self-sabotage.

You do not deserve to blame yourself. You were hurt enough by the narcissist—there is no reason to add to it in this manner. Instead, turn your attention to something else that could be productive. Instead of dwelling further, you may be able to find something else that you can do with your time.

Improve Yourself

When you have time on your hands that you need to burn to keep yourself from dwelling, the best thing that you can do is invest it in yourself. When you invest that time on yourself, you can make it productive instead. You allow yourself to learn something new. You take your bad situation and turn it into something good.

What you do with yourself is up to you. No matter what it is, it is symbolic. Your escape of the abusive situation is affording you a chance to better yourself in some way, shape, or form. The narcissist may have intentionally kept holding you down to make sure that you felt like you could never actually do anything. He may have laughed at your desire to go to school for a new career. He may have told you that you are terrible at cooking when you said that you wanted to learn how to bake cakes. He may have told you that you were a failure when you told him that you wanted to start a small business. He had no interest in you bettering yourself because if you had managed to pull it off, your success would have been a direct threat to him. He would have felt like your success was a challenge, a threat that he was not as good as he claimed. He wanted you to avoid bettering yourself for this very reason—he would be able to keep his power over you.

This means, then, that when you do succeed in bettering yourself somehow, you can acknowledge that you did work hard. You can acknowledge that you did it in the face of adversity, despite the narcissist's negative assumptions. You recognize that you did something worthy, and you will hopefully have something to show for it, whether that is a degree, a new skill, a business, or anything else. Bettering yourself is never a waste of your time.

Focus on Self-Care

When you have been in a narcissistic relationship, you grow accustomed to dumping excessive amounts of your time into someone else. You were dedicated to trying to appease the narcissist, who was never satisfied, leaving you endlessly working to do so. When you finally break free, however, you have plenty of free time to keep you thinking about whether you made the right choice in the first place. After all, the narcissist spent the entire relationship, making you doubt yourself—of course, you would continue to do so at this point.

When you shift that free time that you would usually use to deliberate over your decision onto yourself, you can begin to spend time caring for yourself. This is probably foreign to you after a long relationship—you got used to attending to someone else's needs before meeting your own needs when you were in a relationship with the narcissist. You spent your time making sure that he was satisfied, and you did not spend time to take care of yourself because he was never satisfied in the first place.

Write Down the Reasons Why You Left

One final way you can resist returning to the narcissist may be one of the most powerful ones. You will be making a list of all the reasons that you chose to leave the narcissist and ensuring that you have them for easy access if you ever do feel like you are in a moment of weakness. You will be thinking about the entirety of your relationship with the narcissist, recording what he did, how you felt, and why you should refuse to go back.

Think back to when you realized that you were, in fact, ready to leave. You decided that you were no longer willing or able to accept the abuse in your life. You decided at that moment that you deserved happiness and to escape from the abusive tendencies once and for all. What was that moment? What happened then that made you come to this realization? Why should you avoid ever returning to the narcissist?

It is best to do this step when you are newly out of the relationship, and while the pain of what happened to end the relationship is still fresh in your mind. No matter what that final straw that broke the camel's back was, write it down. Email it to yourself. Scan it and keep it on your phone. Print out a copy to print and put on your mirror that you see every morning to remind you of what happened.

When you have had time to begin to recover from what happened and your emotions fade, you are more likely to start wondering if you made the right decision, and when that happens, you want to have the reason that you left written right in front of you. You will also want to dictate other abusive tendencies that the narcissist had, what he did, and how it made you feel.

You will then want to read this, every single time that you start feeling like returning to the narcissist may not be that bad. When you start feeling like returning would be okay, and that you would rather have the narcissist present than not at all, you want to spend time reading this letter to yourself. Let it be your sort of guide to understanding why you want to avoid returning. It is like your map that clearly shows what has happened and where you will be going from there. It will keep you grounded and firm in your decision. All you must do is remember to read it when you start to doubt yourself.

Chapter 19:
Healing From Narcissistic Abuse if Not Codependent

Y ou have been to hell, but how do you get back from there? What does your future look like? Can you destroy the trauma bond that you have become addicted to? What does it look like to be on the other side? Can you ever feel like yourself again?

These questions and more can come to the surface when you first manage to break away from your abuser. Life can seem strange and scary. You will feel yearnings to go back to your old relationship, even though you know all the reasons you should not.

For some people, the road to healing is not just about healing themselves but also about healing in their relationships and for their partner. There is a way to do this as well—it is hard, but not impossible. You can get there with work, dedication, and leaning on others for help.

Do not make the mistake of trying to do all of this on your own. There is no shame in seeking help. If you are standing at a crossroads and asking yourself: "Well, what is next for me?"

How can you heal after being subjected to a relationship with a narcissist?

Your recovery is an involved process. You know what abuse looks like from a narcissist, and you have explored the details behind the narcissist's history. You have learned who the narcissist is, what their masks are like, how they manipulate you, and you have discovered what has been happening to you. You need to learn these signs and be able to identify the signals so that you can prevent yourself from being placed back into a situation like this.

Healing takes time and effort. You need to learn about yourself before you can heal the damage your narcissist caused. For example, you need to learn about your childhood trauma that has made you susceptible to caring for a narcissist as well as learning how to create and establish boundaries that we need to make others adhere to. You need to understand that you are also accountable for your actions and the behaviors that you portray. This is all you will learn on your path to healing to find peace and a way forward after your traumatic ordeal.

Yes, the narcissist's behavior was terrible, but you need to analyze the other half of the equation as well—yourself. Ask yourself hard to answer questions like why did you stay, why did you allow the ill-treatment to go on for so long? Do not ask these questions to blame yourself, but just to analyze your behaviors. You are not to blame for the situation, but you need to understand how and why you stayed in an abusive situation. Or even why do you continue to stay, if you have not left your narcissist.

If your narcissist fails to get help, you need to make peace because they will never truly take accountability for the emotional turmoil, they put you through. This is merely due to the way their mind works. So, you need to find closure for yourself without expecting it from your partner or ex-partner.

You will go through several stages on your journey to healing.

Stage One: Victim

When you first learn of everything you have been subjected to and realize that your partner is a narcissist, you will probably be feeling victimized. This is because you are coming to terms with the betrayal that your narcissist has created. The feelings that you have pent up inside you that add to this feeling of victimhood are:

- Hurt

- Denial

- Rejection

- Confusion

- Shame

- Victimization by family members or friends that say you are crazy for your beliefs about your partner

- Anger at your narcissist

- Anger at yourself for not realizing or knowing

- Outrage over the love that you gave

- Anger over the time that you spent in the narcissist's cycle

- Fear of what your next step will be

- Fear of being in an unfamiliar new reality

- Feelings of abandonment

- Feeling lonely

These feelings are all going to run through your mind as you break ties with your narcissist or seek to change the behavior. It is a process as you have also become addicted to the way they treat you. You need to be prepared to learn about your narcissist and yourself. Once you have looked introspectively into your past and feelings, you need to study what factors made you their target. How did you allow them to creep into your life, and how did you become accustomed to the abuse? Write these questions down and try your best to answer them objectively.

Stage Two: Survivor

Once you get through your feelings of being a victim and the shock of realizing what was happening to you, you will begin to feel like a survivor. You have a mental shift during this time. Your feeling will change towards:

- Rebuilding your life

- Seeking out a counselor

- Being unwilling to forgive your narcissist

- Trying to find your way back to your old self

- Navigating through your issues of trust

- Learning how to understand yourself and participating in self-care

- Re-evaluating and changing friendships as necessary

- Your anger diminishes

- You feel hope

- A trigger could make you feel angry or depressed

- Discovering your trauma from childhood

- Creating awareness for the flags of a narcissist

At this point in your healing, you will need to actively instill change in your life. This is where the real legwork of your recovery begins.

Before you do anything, you need to learn how to create boundaries and set limits that you do not want someone else to cross. This is how you begin taking your life back. Once you have established your boundaries, stop hiding.

Get back into routine and habits with your friends and family. Go out and have fun. Rediscover the freedom and joy that life can give you.

You might be struggling with forgiveness, that is not unusual, but you need to work on it. Your forgiveness is a pivotal step in your recovery. This act is not for your abuser, but entirely for you. You need to let go of their control over your emotions and actions.

Stage Three: Surviving and Thriving

This is the stage where you have laid the foundation for your healing, and now you need to continue to build and work on it. You might be feeling troubled during your recovery, and some initial feelings of anger and resentment might surface.

- Feelings of anger toward the person that abused you

- Unable to shake the emotions from your past

- Shame and embarrassment at having been the victim of a narcissist

- Lack of concentration in your life at work or even when part of a group setting

- Feeling like you cannot move forward into your new life

- Feeling bitter at the idea of forgiving your abuser

- Conscious of what other people might think as they see you struggle to move on

- Desire to move on and create dreams and live in freedom

It is difficult to process what happened to you and to clear your mind to move forward. You need to refocus your perspective. You must learn about the dangers of keeping your emotional attachment with an abuser that you left. There is the power to be found from releasing your abuser. Your focus needs to be on your recovery, not on the narcissist.

Find the self-confidence you are missing. There was before your narcissist grabbed hold of you. Your confidence will help you move forward. Through your confidence, you should strive to learn to love yourself. By loving yourself completely, you can wash away the chaos and anxiety that your narcissist left with you.

Change is important. With these steps, you can reclaim some of your former self back while also forging a new identity for yourself. Learn to be mindful. Place yourself in every moment and be awake and active during it. As you practice mindfulness, your focus will keep bringing you to present moments, and you will be able to let go of the memories that keep surfacing from the past.

When you are ready, you can start building up healthy relationships. If you have let go of friends during your recovery, try to cultivate new and authentic relationships that offer you support.

Chapter 20:
Healing Process

When you are attempting to heal from the narcissist after escaping, you will need to find ways to take care of yourself somewhere during the determination stage. You need to recover all the wounds that the narcissist's abuse left behind to become the person you are meant to be. Healing can be incredibly difficult if left to your own devices, and you may even feel tempted to move on without ever addressing the harm you endured.

However, it is essential. You will never truly heal if you leave the wounds to fester and worsen. Your sense of self, your happiness, and you, yourself, will slowly wither away if you do not treat the wounds. Just as you know, you must heal a physical wound; you must care for your mental and emotional wounds. Take the time to absorb the methods of healing from abuse and put effort into bettering yourself. You will feel so much relief after you have taken the time to heal.

Only by healing all the wounds you can truly remove all the chains the narcissist has installed and free yourself.

Compassion

As there is an entire stage in the healing process called compassion, it comes as no surprise that it plays a part in healing from your abuse. Remember to have compassion for yourself to acknowledge that you did not deserve the abuse you endured and recognize that making mistakes is okay.

Victims of narcissistic abuse struggle to be compassionate or patient with themselves. They feel as though they are underserving of that compassion, even if they would tell anyone else in their shoes that it is okay, and that compassion is necessary. Even little things can set off a victim of abuse, such as spilling a glass of milk. If you have endured abuse, you may tell yourself that you are stupid for making such a simple mistake, and you may even belittle yourself, calling yourself a fool and worthless.

The problem is, those are not your words—it's the narcissist's. Spilling a glass of milk is not a big deal in the grand scheme of things. In terms of a mistake, it is harmless. Even if the glass shattered, no one died. There was no irreparable damage to anything other than a glass, that most likely does not have some immense value anyway.

Remember to regard yourself with the same compassion you have always had for others. You deserve it just as much as the people you treat with that compassion and directing some of that inward does not take away from anyone else either. The compassion and willingness to forgive yourself will go a long way.

That compassion should also come with patience. It will take time for yourself to heal from the narcissist's abuse, but that does not invalidate you. That does not make you less valuable, and it does not say anything about your worth. It means that you are a human, and you are likely to have roadblocks from time to time. Just because you trip and fall and make a mistake does not mean you should berate yourself or make yourself feel worse.

Allow Yourself Time to Grieve Properly

Grief is a natural part of living in which people cope with loss. Typically, grief is reserved for people who have lost a close family member or friend. As you go through the stages of separating yourself from an abusive relationship, you go through a similar process. This is because, particularly when involved with a narcissist, you have lost someone. You have lost the person you thought the narcissist was.

Remember how the narcissist used a persona to draw you in—you fell in love with the narcissist's mask. You initially loved someone who turned out to be a figment of your abuser's imagination. However, the process of watching the narcissist morph from a perfect lover into a monster is devastating. It is not unlike watching someone fade away from a terminal illness, slowly losing him—but when you lose the narcissist's persona, you are left with a monster wearing your loved one's face as a constant reminder of what you lost.

You still lost someone that you loved, and you should not minimize that. Grief comes in five stages: denial, anger, bargaining, depression, and acceptance.

Creating Healthy Outlets

You have probably developed some pretty toxic thoughts and feelings yourself when you have suffered through narcissistic abuse. Many of these come from what is likely a tendency toward being empathetic, as that is one of the things the narcissist desires most, and you absorbed the narcissist's toxic feelings. Empaths are particularly prone to internalizing the feelings and tendencies of those around them, and the tendencies of the narcissist can be particularly toxic to the empath.

One of the best things to do when you have internalized all that negativity is finding a creative, healthy outlet. You should seek out some way to eliminate the toxicity from you, whether through art, music, learning, taking classes, or anything clsc that appeals to you. Exercising is a common tactic used in which you sweat out the negativity. The important part here is that you manage to eliminate it somehow and that you feel better after you have finished whatever you have chosen to do. Over time, you will release all the pent-up negativity, and you will begin to feel much better about yourself.

Therapy

Therapy can guide you toward healing as well. As briefly touched upon, a therapist is one of the greatest favors you can do for yourself. There are very few people in this world who would not benefit from therapy, and the likelihood of one of them being you are incredibly slim. The sooner you start it, the sooner you will start seeing results. Several different kinds of therapy could be useful for a victim of narcissistic abuse. Through treatment, you will be able to learn valuable skills such as how to deal with the trauma left behind, understand what made you vulnerable to the narcissist in the first place, and how to solve all the problems that come with all the emotions you feel whirling inside of you.

If therapy is something that sounds like it would benefit you, try speaking to your primary care doctor for a referral or seek out recommendations local to your area online. Even if the cost is an issue, there are plenty that will help you on a sliding scale and online options that may be more affordable for you.

Chapter 21:
Techniques to Recover

When you have emotional trauma, it becomes difficult for you to control your emotions. When in this state, the trauma survivor is left vulnerable that the slightest physical, sensory, and emotional cues cause panic as it reminds them of the abuse and trauma.

During this time, the body and mind activate the same way as if exposed to an existing threat. It feels confusing and terrifying to the trauma survivors when they experience this. Learning some grounding and self-soothing techniques help to regulate the emotions when panic sets in.

When you try these techniques, you can feel safer now as it enhances your calm state.

Benefits of Grounding Techniques

When you feel intense anxiety or emotions threaten to overwhelm you, grounding techniques help you remain in the present moment. Doing this will allow you to feel in control and know that you are safe, not back to the abuse.

Staying in the moment means you must focus on the physical world and the sensations you feel right now. You can use these skills whenever your emotions are wild or distressed after your emotions were triggered. During this situation, you become stressed by being caught up with the problematic thoughts and memories of your past encounters with the narcissist.

Reliving bad experiences can make you feel afraid, leading to the development of negative habits. Some of those habits include drinking, binge eating, sleeping, and addictions. These are opposites of healing, which you can prevent from happening through grounding techniques.

How to Do a Grounding Technique

It is easy to perform a grounding technique. When you feel panic or overwhelming emotions, focus on an aspect or sensation of the physical world. For instance, touch the ground or hold the hands of your friend. The impressions you get from these will focus on the internal thoughts and feelings that plague your mind.

When it comes to grounding techniques, you must always practice. Doing this helps you calm down naturally after getting upset. When performing your grounding skills, you must focus on the external experience or the outward appcarancc to let your negative feelings go. Practice different techniques to find out which one works well with you.

Some of the grounding techniques you can try include:

Physical Techniques

- Put your hands in the water, feeling its temperature from your fingertips to the backs of your hands. Try using warm water first, then cold water next. The alternating temperature helps you stay grounded.

- Hold an ice cube in your hands and feel the sensation as it starts melting. Ice cubes are excellent tools to use for grounding techniques with its coldness. It is particularly helpful when dealing with intense feelings.

- Touch or pick up items near you whenever you feel distressed or disassociated. Concentrate on whether it is light or heavy, soft or hard, or warm or cool to the touch. Guessing their colors based on the texture is also an excellent exercise.

- Take a short walk, focusing on your steps. You can concentrate on the feeling as you walk on the ground or silently count your steps. You may also take notice of your footsteps' rhythm each time you put down and lift your foot again.

- Deep breathing is also a grounding technique that helps you keep calm. Take a deep breath, slowly inhaling and exhaling while simultaneously thinking 'in' and 'out.' Feel your lungs getting filled with breath and the air getting pushed back out.

- Perform some exercises or stretches such as jumping up and down jogging, or other similar activities that move different muscle groups. Notice how each movement makes you feel, keeping your focus on it.

- Savoring each bite of food or drink with you enjoying how they taste and smell. Let the flavors linger on your tongue. Concentrate on them to keep your thoughts away from your intense emotions.

- Take a seat or keep standing. Either way, you can stay now whenever you experience traumatic episodes by focusing on the awareness your body feels. Notice each sensation from head to toe. From the coldness of the glass you hold in your hand to the straight posture, you keep your back.

- Listen to your surroundings. The barking of the dogs, the chirping of the birds, each grunt of a machine working, or the gentle thud of footsteps around you. Focus on the conversations you hear, the sounds of the rain pit patting on the roof. All of these help you stay in the moment and not get lost in your painful memories.

Mental Techniques

- Consider one or two categories, such as mammals, places, girl's names, etc. and mentally list them. List as many items, or things you can think about that belongs to every category you included in the mental exercise.

- Try playing a memory game by looking at a detailed picture such as a cityscape for a few seconds. Take in all details of the photo then put it face down while you recreate it in your mind. Recreate it as much as possible, or you can list in your mind all the things you can remember.

- Recite a song, poem, quotes, book passages, or anecdotes, anything you can remember. Do this in your head while visualizing each word or silently mouthing it to yourself while shaping every word in your mouth?

- You can exercise mentally with numbers, such as by reciting the multiplication table. You can also count from 1 to 100 or backward. Simple addition or subtraction problems are great as well.

- Visualization is an excellent grounding technique you can use in varying circumstances. You can visualize your surroundings, something you like to do like a daily task, maybe, or the way your painful feelings leaving you behind.

Self-Soothing Skills

Learning some self-soothing skills can also help you stay calm and relaxed when reeling from the memory of narcissistic abuse. By soothing, it means to regulate your consuming feelings, so you are back to yourself again. The idea is the same when your parents pat your back while you cry.

Only this time, you do it to yourself. There is a bit of a disadvantage with self-soothing, as you might use addictive behavior as a quick fix. It makes it crucial that you choose healthy things to help you cope with your trauma as self-soothing skills.

Use Positive Associations

The use of positive associations created while performing said grounding exercises could also help you with traumatic episodes. Use cue objects, words, or scents that you have associated with good or safe memories. When you see them or hold them while having an attack, they will remind you that you're safe.

Opposite positive associations, you can use distancing techniques when the cues you made began to have negative associations. These techniques will guide your cues back to safe visualizations. Both techniques may be enhanced when performed with meditation.

Deep Breathing

Breathing exercises have been known to be helpful when you need to calm down. When your emotions are overwhelming, focus on your breath so you can induce relaxation and centering. When you take a deep breath and release it, think of your stressors getting released with every exhalation.

While doing breathing exercises, you may indulge in some meditation or listen to soothing music as a background—both help keep you calm. Thanks to the music, you can stop distracting thoughts from entering your mind.

Containment Exercises

Whenever you feel pain because of intense emotions, you can use containment exercises to separate yourself from these feelings until you are ready to deal with them. With these exercises, you can regain your emotions as they allow you to choose when and where to process them freely.

Containment exercises are a lot like mental exercises. Visualize in your mind an actual container—strong and large—enough to safely hold all your traumatic experiences and painful memories. The container is tightly sealed, which can only be opened when you think it is safe.

The container serves as your locker where you can keep negative emotions throughout the day. You put them inside the box and wait until you dare to examine and process your hidden emotions. With this exercise, you can avoid becoming overwhelmed by anxiety, fear, and dissociation.

Chapter 22:
Building Daily Positive Behaviors

T o continue your journey toward healing and to free yourself from the narcissist, you may feel times where you need some extra self-care or quietness to focus on yourself and reflect on everything. When this happens, and you feel the need to seek out quietness, you should try using one of the methods.

Meditations, mantras, and positive affirmations can all be quite beneficial as you attempt to heal from the narcissist, and they can help you in moments of weakness or self-doubt when you are not sure if you are doing the right thing. Through these methods, you will be able to return yourself to a peaceful state of calmness that can aid you in returning to a state of relaxation and clear-headed.

Meditation

Meditation happens when you focus on positiveness. You seek to center yourself in a feeling of positiveness to drown out the negative emotions. If you are feeling upset about the abuse you have endured and are feeling unworthy due to the damage, worried that you will never find someone who wants to be with you because you feel that you are too broken ever to be a viable partner. It is, in a sense—your negative thoughts and feelings are spiraling out of control, and you are struggling to reel them in.

When you meditate, you instead attempt to quiet your mind by focusing on something positive. Rather than feeling unlovable, you may focus on the feeling of being in love and loving yourself. You let yourself shift from that negative place to one rooted in positiveness, in which you feel yourself relaxing.

Over time, you may begin to feel as though you are lovable, and you recognize that you love yourself, which means you must be lovable. Ultimately, the goal when you attempt to meditate is to shift your mind from the negative thought cycles and patterns to positive ones. When you practice, it is easier to change to that quiet place in your mind where you feel calm and safe, even in the face of danger or your greatest fears.

As you come out of your meditative state, dedicate the positive feelings you have created, and that positive energy generated, to yourself and those you love, wishing them the best. Remember those feelings to ground yourself when you feel stress or to guide yourself through your day, making sure the actions you choose are relatcd to thc emotions you generated during meditation.

Mantras

Mantras are quite related to meditation—they are words that you use to keep yourself concentrated on your meditations. They allow you to regroup and focus back on your meditations if you were to get distracted. When you are trying to heal from narcissistic abuse, you can use these mantras to redirect your mind when you are beginning to feel distracted or overwhelmed. When feelings of negativity, worthlessness, or just hurt are threatening to overwhelm you, it is difficult to get out of that rut. You may feel that you have no way to get out of the situation, and when that happens, you can repeat a phrase, or a mantra, to yourself to regroup.

Creating a mantra is an immensely personal task. It can be quite challenging to do if you do not know what you are doing, or you are unsure how to create something significant to you and your situation. When you are ready to create your mantra, take a journal or a sheet of paper and a pen and find a quiet location where you can focus for the next thirty minutes without distractions. This is the most effective when you do it in the morning when your mind is not yet overwhelmed with the dozens of worries you may feel throughout your day. First, begin by identifying something that you will need a mantra for. For the narcissistic abuse survivor, this may be something about healing, self-worth, or self-esteem. You should then focus on that one thing that you want to attain. If you wish to achieve healing, you may think about those healing feelings you felt when meditation and how you want to be able to return to that state of calmness. Write in your journal about everything and anything that comes to mind regarding healing from the abuse. Take thirty minutes to free-write without distraction.

If you wrote about how you want your mind to heal from the narcissist's abuse, you could write something along the lines: "I am ready to let go of the pain and welcome happiness and loving energy into my life."

You can then use this in moments of stress when those feelings from the abuse threaten to overwhelm you and attempt to integrate them into your meditations. The more you use them in conjunction with your meditations, the more you may begin to feel as though they are becoming associated with the feelings of calmness and healing you were feeling during your meditation.

Example:

Take things at your own pace: When you have lived a life of being abused by the narcissist when you do not tend to his needs immediately after he has asked for you to do so, you may attempt to move quicker than necessary. You are trying to compensate for the fact that he may want multiple things that also clash with you meeting your own needs. Because of this, you may have gotten into the habit of rushing yourself. A mantra such as this one reminds you that it is okay to slow down sometimes. It reminds you to be mindful of what is happening around you and to take things at a natural pace rather than forcing things to go quicker than necessary.

I am not ashamed of myself: Frequently, narcissistic abuse victims find themselves hiding. The narcissist does not want the outside world to see who they are because they fear the judgment they may face. You may try to hide your pain behind a brave face, hiding your abuse and attempting to minimize the effects the narcissist may have had on you. However, this defeats the entire purpose of healing—you can be you, even if the you that you are right now is injured and in need of healing. Do not be ashamed to show your scars. They are the marks that you have survived, and you should be proud of them, not ashamed.

Positive Affirmations

Affirmations are sentences you speak to yourself to remind you to take a certain mindset or action for positive daily behaviors. Like the mantra, they are short and personalized, but rather than encompassing a goal or desired result, the affirmations are triggers to act or think in a certain way that is conducive to positivity. When spoken to yourself, preferably out loud, so you hear the words, these affirmations aid in shifting how you are thinking at that moment and empower you.

These affirmations are like support for the foundations of your mind—they keep you strong in moments of weakness, and over time, the more you repeat them to yourself, the more real they become to you now. Over time, you will find yourself less vulnerable to the negativity that you had tried to protect yourself against in the first place. You will find yourself needing to rely on the affirmations less and less during your journey toward healing.

When you are trying to create your affirmations, they must follow a specific structure. They must be:

- Positive: All statements must be worded positively to reinforce the idea that you will be shifting your thinking into positivity.

- Present tense: Your affirmation must be in the present tense to make it more difficult to deny or reject. By wording things positively, you are saying that they are valid at that moment.

- Brief and specific: Your affirmation should be short, but specific to whatever it is that you are attempting to correct within yourself. Short means it is easier for you to remember now, while specific means you should be able to use it for its intended purpose.

- About you: You are the only thing in this world that you have control over. As such, you should make sure your affirmation focuses on you when you make it. You will be able to say that it is true because you can make it so.

Example:

I am healing, even if it is a slow process: This reminds you that you are working toward achieving health and wellness. You are actively working to better yourself and heal, and even when you feel as though you are not, or that you have taken a step backward, or failed in some way, this affirmation will remind you that you are a work-in-progress, and that is okay. It is okay for the healing process to be slow. It is okay for you to have setbacks sometimes.

I am trustworthy, and I am willing to rely on my perceptions of reality: Remember how the narcissist loves to gaslight victims? It can be incredibly useful to remind yourself that you are trustworthy, even if the narcissist has attempted to convince you otherwise. Whenever you are beginning to doubt whether you understand what is happening, you can repeat this affirmation to yourself.

I can support my boundaries, and I am protecting them any time they are challenged: This reminds you to protect your limitations. Remember, boundaries are created to make some distance between yourself and another person to protect yourself. If you are protecting your boundaries, you are essentially insisting that they are honored, and your limits are protected. This can be difficult after having lived with a narcissist that would frequently push back at your boundaries and refuse to respect them.

I am prioritizing my self-care: This reminds you that sometimes, you need to put yourself first. Sometimes, it is appropriate and essential to tell other people no and tend to yourself. Your self-care keeps your mind and body happy and healthy. Ultimately, you are responsible for yourself, and you need to take that responsibility seriously because no one else will do it for you. Even if the narcissist has taught you to fear to care for yourself, it must be done for your own sake and for any who may rely on you for care, such as children or pets.

Chapter 23:
Therapy

Cognitive Behavioral Therapy (CBT)

A patient affected by narcissism often shows self-lost behavior, presenting signs of withdrawal from others, low self-esteem, fear of rejection, and negatives self-perception. These signs are strategies a patient employs to cope with past traumatic experiences or compensate for what was lost or denied. The copying strategies might cause more harm to the affected person.

Cognitive-behavioral therapy aims to help the individual affected by narcissism to change the harmful copying strategies and adopt strategies that help the patient redeem himself or herself gradually. This method is not sometimes easy if the patient is not ready to open and share the doctor's traumatic experiences. Therefore, the doctor should be more skilled in bringing the patient to feel comfortable to share the experiences.

It involves the doctor building trust and providing a friendly environment that lets the patient relieve all the emotions that have built up over the years. In some instances, the patient does not understand why he or she shows certain behaviors, and the help of a person who was close during the traumatic experiences is needed.

After the confession of the past events that affect the present life, the patient should be allowed to suggest ways to forget the past. At this point, the doctor should be careful not to impose strategies that the patient is not comfortable but should give guidance to make sure that the suggestions are more adaptive and positive.

Cognitive Behavioral therapy is not time-bound, because the progress from one stage to another or length of a given stage depends on the patient; the essential aspect is the internal resolution and reconciliation of the past and the present. The main goal is that the patient achieves an inner balance and discovers himself and herself. There is also a sense of empathy, which helps the patient to understand why and how the events happen as they did in the past. This stage is also meant to make the patient develop skills such as self-regulation and resilience.

Eventually, the patient corrects the faulty interpretations about the people and environment around and replaces them with more rational and accurate explanations. Therefore, the patient can understand that the environment gives what you give it and starts to engage in behavior that gives more positive experiences leading to stable behavioral and emotional reactions that are not harmful and exaggerated.

Therapy for Complex

Some patients suffer from complex narcissism that poses severe challenges for therapists and other supporting professionals. Such patients have experienced traumatic events at an early age, and the events become repetitive so that they control their lives completely. Others have experienced multiple situations that have progressively destroyed their inner being, thus affecting their interpersonal relations. Examples of such events might include abandonment, antipathy, neglect, betrayal, exploitation, rejection, and abuse. All the mentioned experiences become more complex if they started at the early stages of development of a child because they affect the healthy growth in all aspects, leading to negative beliefs about others and more so self.

Patients with such extreme and accumulated trauma are often troubled, and experience feelings of shame, loneliness, confusion, low self-esteem, distrust, anger, alienation, and grief. The patients have difficulties getting along with others, fitting in, and getting close to others is always a problem, even if they try. Therapy for complex aims at offering effective regulation, improving body image, create relationships and attachment, and control impulses.

The patient should be helped to develop awareness of his or her emotions and tolerance. Patients also need to be guided on how to establish relationships and attachments. Therapy complex helps the individual understand themselves and the world around; the patients may disconnect themselves from relationships because they fear harm, but if guided, they may reconsider their views on the importance of creating a relationship and engaging in collaborative engagements. They slowly achieve integration in society and increase engagement with others.

Cognitive Processing Therapy

This method of treatment is related to cognitive behavior therapy (CBT). It is most effective in patients that have experienced traumatic events that affect their thinking about themselves and their environment. Such patients particularly have issues related to safety; they doubt their ability to protect themselves or those around them. Trust is also an issue for they question their judgment of other people and their intentions, and therefore, they lack control of their own lives and often are unable to influence the lives of those close to them. Their social life might be complicated as they cannot easily connect with people and accept them. These thoughts lead to fear, anger, guilt, and anxiety.

The Cognitive processing Therapy concentrates equipping the patient with skills and help to challenge negative thoughts and see how they affect their life. Mostly, it is used in patients that have been diagnosed with Post-Traumatic Stress Disorder, and not recommended for patients who have literacy difficulties because it involves the use of written work and writing. The therapy can be conducted in group sessions or individual sessions.

The Education Phase

During the education phase, the therapist builds a rapport with the affected person, which should be done briefly to reduce the chances of the patient changing his mind about the therapy. The patient is then educated about narcissism and how it is caused, the effects of traumatic events on one's life, and strategies people use to cope. The therapist also provides a rationale for treatment, presents the course of treatment, and gives effective treatment guidelines. The guidelines include compliance in terms of attendance and completion of all assignments given out of the therapy session.

Processing the Events and Their Meaning

This session begins with the patient writing down the accounts of the past events and how they have affected him or her. It helps to discover the stuck points that hinder the patient from living a normal life. Stuck points can also be identified through probing with questions like, what were your thoughts. Why did you react that way? At this point, the therapist also identifies the patients' thinking patterns and changes in emotions that would guide in a successful change of negative thoughts and emotions.

Replacing Harmful Thoughts

Like in the case of Cognitive Behavior Therapy, it helps the patient to understand why the events took that course and accept that it was not their fault. The process of taking control of the present and future thoughts without the influence of the past sets in transforming a narcissist to a normal person.

Prolonged Exposure Therapy

This type of treatment is derived from the traditional exposure therapy for those who feel anxious when faced with situations. An individual is repeatedly exposed to an anxiety-evoking situation until he or she overcomes the anxiety or fear. Patients experiencing narcissism have experienced events that have caused a change in behavior such as low self-esteem, withdrawal from peer groups, and feeling unsafe. People with experiences of traumatic events tend to avoid situations that remind them of the trauma. Avoiding the thoughts or situations arouses the memories to maintain the narcissism, and the patient cannot move on.

Prolonged exposure helps the patient to stop the avoidance and confronts the thoughts and situations that bring back the memories of a traumatic event experienced. The therapy involves two types of exposure—vivo exposure and imaginal exposure.

Imaginal Exposure

In the imaginal exposition, the therapist asks the patient to revisit traumatic events through imagination. The therapist talks with the patient to allow him to describe the events in the imagination aloud. The memory is repeated during successive therapy sessions, and the duration is prolonged. The repeated and prolonged exposure makes the patient get used to the horrifying event, and anything related to fire does not make him nervous anymore. The patient now develops a new perspective of what happened and why it happened; there is a realization that the memories are not harmful and can handle them. It is also a way of giving the patient a chance to control his or her life, the "I can, and I will" voice gets back.

Vivo Exposure

This type of exposure gives the patient a chance to control real-life situations that he or she considers dangerous. Sometimes people hear stories from others about certain events or are threatened. Vivo exposure allows the patient to gradually approach the situation that brings the memories of the traumatic events, such as fear of walking alone in the park and driving a car. The exposure helps to reduce excessive avoidance and fears after a traumatic event.

It allows the patient to confront the situation and get over the fear. The process is gradual and systematic; the severity of the feared situation increases until the patient is comfortable staying in the situation without fear or anxiety.

Chapter 24:
Alternative Healing Methods

T here are many helpful and potent healing methods you can use to get your life in order after leaving an abusive relationship. Your well-being is essential, so be sure to embrace every opportunity you must heal. If you would like an overhaul of your spirit, soul, mind, and body, the following proven healing techniques can be of significant help.

Eye-Movement Desensitization and Reprocessing (EMDR) Therapy for Narcissist Abuse Recovery

If you need therapy to reduce the physiological distress that comes with traumatic memories, like those from an abusive relationship, EMDR is a good option. This is because it can reduce or even eliminate the after-effect of such recollections. This happens by directing the attention, and the memory, at something else—something other than themselves. You will not have to talk about what is going on in your mind. This relies on stimulating the brain using the immediate surroundings.

EMDR is unique and has been proven effective because victims do not need many sessions before improvement begins. When the eyes move rapidly, it helps open the brain neural network. This allows memories to be processed uniquely in a safe and healthy environment, besides the one responsible for the trauma. The idea is to replace these memories with empowering thoughts and feelings. The end game ensures that such memories do not create anxiety, fear, hatred, depression, and other symptoms of Post-Traumatic Stress Disorder that comes from abuse. As a result, the person is free to embrace life and all it has, even to start a new relationship without fear.

Victims of narcissistic relationships are characterized by tons of negative memories and abuse that can be sexual, verbal, emotional, or physical.

While in an EMDR therapy unit, the victim will have to access and think about one of the memories of such abusive episodes. This happens while they keep their eye on an external stimulus for a couple of seconds.

Emotional Freedom Technique

Another effective strategy to help lessen the traumatizing effects of narcissistic abuse is the emotional freedom technique. It is simple, free, and can be done without a therapist in the comfort of your home. You can also work with a skilled EFT therapist or a friend to help you get through the trauma.

ETF, also known as tapping, involves a technique that all patients must do is tap while concentrating on a problem. EFT teaches that you can tap these specific acupressure points while focusing on the memories of the hurt and trauma from the abuse. With this, you will discover that you can access the memory without the anxiety, allowing the victim to let go of all the negative emotions associated with the relationship's trauma.

Often, when we are anxious and stressed, it is because of unrest and feeling threatened. This is common with victims of narcissistic abuse.

As a result, the trauma and aftermath of a relationship with a narcissist can trigger the same physical response our forefathers had when facing a tiger.

You can calm the body by tapping the endpoints of the meridian. To make this more effective, we recommend tapping while discussing or creating images of the stressful relationship and breakup. This way, the tapping alters the body's response to the images.

Tapping helps balance your energy and expel negative emotions from the body. The natural balanced state of a man, what we were born with, is joy and happiness.

With tapping, you can eliminate tension and emotions blocking the natural balance until there is room for joy and happiness, rather than being held down by the trauma.

Mirror Exposure Therapy

Mirror exposure therapy also helps treat negative self-image, reduce anxiety, and another damaging aftermath of breaking up with a narcissistic partner. It is a pretty effective strategy that enables you to develop self-love and learn to accept yourself. Continuous exposure to criticism and abuse from a narcissist can deal a big blow to one's self-esteem. You will then find yourself doing things to please the narcissistic partner, even if it means changing who you are.

Rather than getting uncomfortable, tensed up, and dissatisfied with who you are (due to the brainwashing from the narcissist), this therapy can help you accept who you are without shame. Mirror exposure therapy aims to suppress and eliminate the unconscious process that makes a reflection of the victim become an object of torture.

Mirror exposure therapy is of tremendous help in this kind of circumstance. Also, this therapy works best when combined with effective management of the emotions and negative thoughts. In other words, to have tangible relief with this therapy, you need to handle this in two processes.

Significant improvement in patients going through mirror work is possible because of the pillars in which the process revolves.

- Readjustment of Self-Interpretation: After a traumatic breakup, the victim might associate everything that goes wrong with the breakup. This therapy helps terminate such prediction while allowing the client to have a healthy interpretation.

- Attention Bias: Over time, the victim might attribute the failure of the relationship to their imperfections. Regret sets in, and they wish they could be better and more tolerant. This therapy helps realign such thoughts with reality.

- Reduction of Anxiety and Fear: Problematic and negative emotions will surge during the breakup. Mirror work helps the patient develop a positive relationship with themselves, such that depression, anxiety, and fear have no way to set in.

Without a doubt, this therapy is a terrific tool in bringing sanity to a victim of narcissistic abuse. All in all, it gives you the courage to accept yourself, be happy, shake off the negative emotions, and prepare yourself for what life has to offer.

Chakra Balancing

Energy healing is a deep practice that triggers the energy system hidden in the body. This helps get rid of blockages, keeps the mind at peace, and brings serenity to your spirit. Breaking through these energy blocks activates the body's ability to heal itself. It is a holistic healing method that encompasses the spirit, soul, and body.

Energy healing employed by chakra healing has its basis in science and ancient principles. Chakra has been proven to heal the deepest wounds and trauma that might arise from any traumatic experience. To understand how to heal with chakra, the concept of the energy body is vital.

At its most basic, the human body is made of energy. By energy body, we mean a system that conveys life force around and through us. This life force energy connects us to the earth, to one another, and the divine. There is this thing in you that knows when someone is toxic when their energy feels good, and when their aura is tranquil.

The energy body has two major components: the aura and chakra systems.

The Aura

The aura is like an electric energy field coming from your body in bubbles. It is like energy layers that come from your chakras. It is seen as colors, based on the vibrations they give.

The body energy is in a constant state of change, based on physical and emotional health. People can feel their energy change, which serves two critical purposes: protection and information exchange.

The aura is like a barrier of energy that stands between you and the environment. A healthy aura provides a sense of security, keeping you from others' energy emanating around you. Your boundary is clear, enabling you to tell the difference between your emotions and needs from those of others.

The Chakras

Various energy centers in the body represent areas of emotional, spiritual, and physical functioning. The body has seven main chakras linked to each other through the energy channels that run through the body. In the body, there is a constant recycling of energetic breath. While new energy comes in, old ones are expelled. With your breath, you can transport energy through your body. The breath serves as a bridge between what we are feeling and what we want to feel.

Art Therapy

There will be various surges of distressing emotions upon ending a narcissistic relationship. It is not uncommon for people in this category to experience anxiety and symptoms of Post-Traumatic Stress Disorder. Art therapy has proven to be reasonably effective in helping people heal from the emotional trauma caused by a narcissistic relationship.

The effect of trauma on the body is overwhelming. It causes both physical and emotional reactions in the victim. It is common for victims to experience disturbing flashbacks, sleep disturbances, panic and anxiety, anger, depression, and guilt. As a result, a person's normal functioning in day-to-day activities might be impaired. Art therapy is an effective treatment that can help restore sanity.

There are times victims of trauma abuse may feel lost. It could be difficult for them to find the right words to express their emotions. This is where art therapy comes in as a rescue to trauma victims when they feel stuck.

Healing and recovery after narcissistic abuse also have to do with reclaiming your body's safety, emotions, and senses. Prolonged exposure to narcissistic abuse can make victims feel disconnected from their bodies. This is due to the constant threat from their abuser, which leads to a feeling of unsafety, and constant fear during the period of the abuse. To fully recover from such injury, victims need to develop new relationships with their bodies. Victims need to be aware of the body's sensations, as well as the mode of interaction of their body with the world around them. Therefore, self-awareness is critical to healing.

Chapter 25:
Practicing Mindfulness

A t its simplest, mindfulness is the idea that, when engulfed in chaos and strong emotions, you can take a moment to detach from the situation at hand and observe what is happening from a rational perspective. You sort of retreat within yourself to reflect on how you are feeling and why you feel the way you are in the hopes of finding answers that can help you better cope with what is bothering you.

This is a particularly useful way to identify any emotional triggers, those things in the outside world that automatically trigger you to feel everything the narcissist has programmed you to feel. There are undoubtedly some left in you after a relationship with a narcissist but learning them all can take plenty of time and patience. When you want to practice mindfulness, you want to understand why you respond the way you are full.

This is a fantastic skill for anyone to have, as mindfulness can help control emotional outbursts and help lessen stress. It is an incredibly healthy coping mechanism and is valuable to learn. Mindfulness involves five steps that will allow you to achieve the state of mindfulness. This state is a state of quiet, internal attentiveness. When you are first learning mindfulness, it is best to do it in quiet periods to master the art before starting to use it when tension builds.

Sit Down

Step 1 in mindfulness is to sit down or identify a quiet place where you can quietly and safely focus on your breathing. Anywhere is acceptable, so long as you can focus and are comfortable, try to find a quiet corner in your home or underneath a tree in your yard. The critical part here is that you need to be calm and relaxed wherever you choose.

Choose a Time

With the goal in mind, choose how long you are willing to dedicate to your first few attempts at mindfulness. Typically, you are better off starting with a shorter period at first and slowly working your way up to longer ones. Perhaps, for your first time, set a goal of 5 minutes of mindfulness.

Pay Attention to Your Body

Choose a comfortable position and focus on your body. You want to choose a position in which you feel stable and relaxed, and that will be comfortable for the duration of your mindfulness. Once you have settled in, really start to focus on your body. Attempt to feel every part of yourself, starting at the tips of your toes and slowly working your way up to the top of your head. You should do this slowly as if you were mentally scanning yourself. Pay attention to any areas that are particularly tense and try to relax them.

Breathe

Focus on your breathing. Take one breath in and try to follow the feeling of it into your lungs, holding it there before exhaling, and repeating. Make sure your breaths are deep, cleansing breaths, and focus on each one.

Keep Your Mind on Track

Any time you feel your mind wandering, quietly put it back on your breathing without judging yourself. Remember how you are supposed to feel compassionate about yourself? Mainly, it is easy to get distracted in the beginning, and that is nothing to be ashamed of. Just regroup and continue.

When completing all the steps, you should feel far more relaxed than when you started. This can be a fantastic tool to unwind after a busy or stressful day or feel your temper rising. As you master being able to call yourself to mindfulness when calm, you can begin using it as a coping mechanism when you feel frustrated or stressed out, or any time you start to debate whether returning to the narcissist would be too bad. Often, those insecurities are tied to some sort of physical distress, and you should try to let them go as best as you can.

Another trick for mindfulness that some people find works well, particularly when emotions are running high is the 5-4-3-2-1 rule. In this technique, you seek to identify things around you with your various senses, engaging them instead of allowing your negative emotion to consume you. When you focus on yourself again, you can manage your reactions in the future.

Sight

First, start by identifying five things around you that you can see. Be as descriptive as possible with yourself if you can be. Perhaps you see a blue ball with a woven texture on the ground, smooth, clear glass on the table next to you, and a sky the color of a clear blue ocean that you dream about vacationing to see. When you have identified five things to yourself, you are ready to move on to your next sense.

Touch

Focus on your sense of touch. Notice four different things around you that you can feel. Perhaps you feel sand giving way beneath your feet, or a cool breeze caressing your hair. Whatever you feel, try to identify four as accurately as possible. Feel each one the best you can and focus on every single detail. Notice how your hair tickles your face when the wind blows it, or how your entire body shifts as the sand does beneath you, compensating for the moving surface.

Hearing

You should then focus on your hearing. Listen for three things around you and take a few moments to hear them. You should pay attention to how they sound, following their melodies and rhythms the best you can. If you hear a bird trilling, focus on how its song rises and falls and how quickly it does.

Smell

Fourth, you will identify two different things around you that you can smell. Do you smell your perfume? What is the scent you have this time? Is it sweet? Do you smell the scents of flowers warming in the sun?

Feeling

Lastly, identify one thing within you that you are feeling at that moment. Are you angry? What is that anger doing to your body? Is it speeding your pulse up? Is it making you tense up? If you are sad, do you feel that hollow feeling spreading in your chest? Are your shoulders hunched? Figure out how you are feeling and how it affects your body.

Disengaging From the Narcissist

Disconnecting from the narcissist will involve going through various stages, much like grieving. This is your process of letting go of the narcissist and recognizing that the relationship is ruined and needs to be ended permanently. Though easier said than done, disengaging and detaching from the narcissist is crucial to healing. Like the stages of grief, you will go through three distinct stages when you are attempting to disengage from the narcissist before finally reaching stage 4: freedom.

Stage 1: Refusing to Take the Blame

In stage 1, you refuse to allow yourself to be blamed for anything that happened. You tell yourself that you did not deserve what the narcissist did, and even though you may have ended the relationship, it was not you that degraded the relationship to the point that it had to be ended. This stage involves you recognizing that the narcissist will never give you what you deserved in the relationship. The narcissist will never be the partner you wanted him to be, and you recognize that. You acknowledge that the narcissist is flawed beyond your ability to repair someone and that his destructive nature is not yours to manage, nor is it something that can be forced upon you. The narcissist becomes someone that you may love still, but you recognize the truth in the situation and that the relationship must end for everyone's sake.

Stage 2: Anger and Resentment

At stage 2, you realize that all the hope you had for the relationship and the narcissist is being replaced. At this stage, you are angry. You see that the narcissist is not the person you wanted, and you begin to resent him. Even if you still have feelings at this stage, you are not likely to act upon them. You refuse to allow the relationship to consume you any longer. At this stage, you no longer care about the manipulation. The narcissist has likely been slinging at you to try to get you back. You recognize that you deserve better than to be treated poorly or with disrespect. You feel the need to stand up for yourself and better yourself. You want to live a life of happiness, not one in which your sole duty is to provide someone else with the joy you have been deprived of feeling for so long.

Stage 3: Detaching and Setting Yourself Free

When you finally hit stage 3, you are finally detaching. The very sight of the narcissist or the mere mention of his name could be enough to make you feel sick to your stomach, and you realize that the love you had for him once upon a time has faded away. You have instead worked on bettering yourself. If you have been going to a therapist or been interacting with a support group, you are beginning to take their advice more frequently and realize that it works. You are far more concerned with getting what you want and need than worrying about the narcissist. You make your decisions based on what is best for you as opposed to anyone else, and for the first time in a long time, you can practically taste freedom.

Stage 4: Freedom

At this point, you are finally free. You no longer allow the narcissist to have any sway on you, and you have likely cut all contact with him. You have completely and utterly separated yourself from the narcissist, and you could never feel better. Your freedom was earned through metaphorical, and quite possibly literal, blood, sweat, and tears, and you plan on enjoying it, no matter what the narcissist has to say about it.

Bettering Yourself

As you continue your journey toward getting over the narcissist, you should put work into yourself. Attempting to better yourself gives you something entirely to focus on, aside from the narcissist, and will keep you busy. You will not have time to worry about the narcissist if you pick up a new hobby, such as learning to play the piano. You can even use this hobby to insert into time that you usually spent with the narcissist.

Ultimately, learning a new skill and bettering yourself can only help you. You will never be worse off if you focus your energy and attention on learning a new skill, but if you use that time to focus on the past, dwell, and mope, you are likely to feel guilty about it later. Overall, it just makes more sense for you to spend that time focusing on things that will better you or can give you some new sense of self-worth to replace the damage the narcissist has done.

Chapter 26:
Change Your Mindset

S uccess and happiness are all about our mindsets. It affects everything in our lives, even how we react and handle the world around us. If you want to stop being codependent on the person you have a relationship with, you must train your brain and the rest of you to either stop being codependent or become independent. To achieve your goals, you need your mindset to level up with your aspirations.

The Path to Self-Improvement

Your self-talk has a direct connection with whether you have a positive or negative mindset. Consider changing your negative self-talk into a full-on empowerment speech. Your mindset is also a reflection of how you see yourself. If you continuously believe, for example, that you're a slob or a bad worker, you will eventually train your brain into believing and following these thoughts. Through reading, you might be surprised at how quickly you pick up on the author's way of thinking. You may find that books help you feel more positive, depending on their genres and titles. Go for self-motivating and happy books and take note of how much your mindset changes by journaling.

Reading is an excellent activity to take up due to their ability to see how others feel and think. Using your environment to exercise your way of thinking is maybe one of the best options. We tend to forget that there is a lot more out there than little old us when trapped in a certain mindset. You might think you're stuck in the worst situation possible until you see someone else in an even worse predicament than yourself. Nature can be your getaway and "mind cleanser" when you need it. There is nothing like beautiful scenery to readjust your way of thinking and make you appreciate the beauty of this world and life.

Once your head is clear again, you can carry on with your self-improvement journey. Sometimes all we need is a bit of a break from our minds to get back on track. There's no better break than a walk-in nature. Surround yourself with people with your desired mindset and try to celebrate your small daily achievements in life; it will lead you to accomplish many more.

You Are Good Enough

Everyone has a moment where they felt like they weren't good enough. Worse than that, I believe all of us have let the words and thoughts of others dictate how we feel about ourselves. You oversee your feelings and thoughts. A perfect example of what can make us feel like we're not good enough is the opinions of others and that little voice. Shut down your inner critic. The moment that little voice starts nagging at you about something that makes you feel inferior shut it down.

Shift your focus onto something else or just simply saying "no," you are training yourself to recognize your self-worth. Make a list of what boosts your confidence when you can't get rid of that voice. Perhaps you should consider saving or writing down messages that someone said that put a smile on your face. If they're truly worth it, stick them up somewhere you'll see them often, like the bathroom mirror.

It is easy to compare ourselves to others daily as we always want to be the best that we can be. The hard truth is that there is always going to be someone better than you. There will always be someone smarter, faster, or more attractive. You need to make peace with it, or it will eat you up inside. You don't need to be better than everyone else. You only need to be you.

Do things that make you happy and make you feel good. Compliment that stranger on their shoes if you want to. If you make them feel good, you're bound to make yourself feel even better. Just be kinder to yourself and know that being human is about being flawed. It's not something to put yourself down over.

Social media is one of the things that is a major cause of people not feeling good enough about themselves. Many of us have at least one social media account, and it is incredibly difficult to avoid, particularly since they are designed to be addictive. We so easily compare ourselves to a picture-perfect life online while completely ignoring the fact that we all have flaws and rough days. Just because someone is more likely to share their fun and exciting days online doesn't mean there aren't bad ones, they don't show you. Let go of the unrealistic idea that everything is perfect for anyone who isn't you.

Stop Procrastinating

Stop procrastinating and make changes. If you want to make changes in your life, it's up to you to do it. Aim for your desired direction of change and go for it. Cut off that toxic person that causes nothing but upset in your life. These are some of the most important first steps to realizing your full self-worth. You know yourself better than anyone, even if it doesn't always feel like it. If you want to do something or your mind tells you to do something, there is probably a good reason for it.

It requires hard work and dedication. To start, pick one personal change that seems most important to you and aim for it. Remember that even baby steps are better than standing still. Write down your progress to keep yourself motivated and to be able to reflect on how far you've come. Be patient. As with all good things in life, it will take time to make these changes, so don't get discouraged when things don't happen immediately. Nobody else will be able to take the first steps for you, but once you begin, you'll realize how much you're worth it.

What habits would you want to change?

- Your habit could be to feel unloved by your partner

- To have a fear of your partner leaving you

- You made jealousy a habit

- Your partner's opinions are more important than yours

- You like to demand your partner, even if it's an unrealistic expectation

- You are aware of how you are acting and reacting, but you tell yourself you cannot change because you were born with these habits

- You pretend things are great because those things are already your habits

- You have become an extremely irritable person who doesn't get along anymore with his or her partner

Chapter 27:
Reconnect With Your True Self

L ife may not be all good for victims who manage to escape narcissistic abuse cycles. Many struggles to heal for years, experiencing intermittent periods of growth and rehabilitation punctuated by episodes of emotional relapse. Recovering victims often report an overwhelming feeling of relief and a surreal sense of calm once they start to get used to the rhythm of their lives under the rules of no-contact with dangerous narcissists.

Even on the painful periods, it's essential for any victim to consistently forgive themselves, appreciate their strength and resilience, and throw themselves enthusiastically into a self-care routine. They must also try to always look towards the future rather than ruminating too heavily on the painful past.

The most insidious legacy of narcissistic abuse is that it attempts to corrupt the victim's ability to enjoy self-esteem, interpersonal love, and all the other beautiful things that an empathetic life can offer, even after the abusive situation has been left behind. The best and most powerful form of revenge you can seek upon a narcissistic abuser is to deny them that possibility. Make the conscious choice to be happy and compassionate; give and receive honest, authentic love with joy and optimism.

Removing narcissism from your life frees you from a lot of toxic nonsense, but it also sometimes means getting rid of your emotional safety net, which can be very scary. Without these dominant personalities around to tell you what to do, how to think, and how to feel, you'll have to decide for yourself, and take responsibility for your behaviors. Reconnecting with your authentic self—the person you were before the abuse rewired your brain—can be a lengthy process, so you might as well dive in and do your best to enjoy it. Ask yourself: what do I like, when no one else tells me what I'm supposed to live?

Where do I want to be? How do I want to feel? How do I want to designate my time?

The most important question to ask yourself is what you want.

Encourage yourself to experiment; try new things and be bold. You may be quite surprised at the person you find underneath all those emotional bruises and baggage once they've been cleared away.

Forgiveness is an essential part of your healing process. But you do not necessarily want to forgive your abuser. Many narcissistic abuse victims are too forgiving of narcissists, which is why they allowed the abuse to last if it did.

You need to forgive yourself and acknowledge that your story's truth has been obscured in your head for a long time; the narcissist was not a good person and did not have your best interests at heart. It was all an act. They knew you were in pain, and instead of releasing you from it, they compounded it at every possible opportunity. You played into this because you wanted to see the best in them. You trusted and believed in them. You did nothing wrong to deserve this treatment. You deserve forgiveness.

But at the same time, on some level, you had to be aware that this relationship was unhealthy and allowed it to continue anyway. You put up with behaviors that you should have walked away from. You made excuses for your abuser and protected them from facing the consequences of their actions. This is where you begin to take personal responsibility for your healing, which is not to be confused with accepting blame for the abuse.

Your goal here is not to make yourself feel bad or convince yourself that you asked for this treatment; on the contrary, your goal is to understand why you allowed the abuse to happen so that you can make better, healthier choices forward. There is no shame in this; usually, we accept abusive behaviors because they come alongside other things that we desperately desire, such as a sense of security, financial empowerment, or simply a feeling of significance. Many of us long to feel needed by someone, and it's that simple desire that leaves us vulnerable to narcissistic abuse. Recognizing your points of vulnerability—the ones that continuously encourage you to ignore the red flags and remain in a toxic relationship—is the best way to guard yourself against future abuse threats.

Finally, you may feel stuck, paralyzed, or pulled in two different directions for quite some time after leaving a narcissistic abuser. Half of your soul will be drifting into the gravitational pull of the past, wanting to revisit memories, explore them, and look for answers. Meanwhile, the other half will be exhausted from this situation and eager to move forward, leaving the abuse behind like a snake shedding its skin. Understand that this dichotomy will tire you out quickly. It may be best to set up designated timeframes to explore the past and the future separately, allowing you to devote your full attention to each and live mindfully in the present.

Eventually, you will reach a point where you can meet new people, and you won't feel the need to explain what you've been through to justify your personality or behaviors. You may not be conscious of it or see it happening, but when you get there, you will have officially freed yourself from the claws of narcissistic abuse. Don't forget your story but recognize this as an opportunity to write a new ending and change the entire narrative. And always remember that the abuse you've suffered through never made you weak—it only served to make you stronger, smarter, and more powerful in the end.

Victims of narcissistic abuse are often haunted by an unfounded sense of shame, even after they've cut ties and moved on from the narcissist who hurt them.

When the relationship is over, the victim is left carrying the shame of the abusive behavior that they tolerated, as well as the shameful fear that they were somehow guilty of the same narcissistic behavior that their abuser displayed. This can impact the victim's future relationships, smothering confidence, and promoting phantom anxiety. If feelings of shame are haunting you, the best thing you can do for yourself is to find a therapist or counselor to help you reframe your memories and rewrite your narrative.

Chapter 28:
Activities to Regain Control

Interacting with Pets

One activity worth considering as you try to regain control over your thoughts is imagining what one's pets are thinking. Pets teach us about nature, life, death, and responsibility.

The neatest thing about this activity is that it urges us to think about thinking. From this activity, you could consider questions as in-depth as asking what the nature of thought is and whether non-human animals do an activity like the one, we call thinking. Your ideas can stay as light as considering why your kitten is looking in a specific direction or what it thinks is beneath the blanket when we put our hand under it.

Trying to understand what kind of interaction a pet wants or requires from its human owner. The benefit of this activity is explicitly examining the individuality of one's pet. This discursive activity is meant to allow you to wonder what your pet wants and expects from you.

Once you've thought about all the things this very different kind of being wants and needs from you, think about how important you are to the different kinds of beings in your life. Think about how much you do for the people in your life. Think about how much effort you put into giving others what they want or expect from you.

Think about how much control you have over that fact. Think about why you do these things for your pet or other people. Think about how it is your choice whether you do something for others. Think about your amount of control in various situations coming to mind.

This activity should continue throughout the life of your pet. Each time something involving the treatment of one's pet comes up; you can return the thought that you are choosing to do something for your pet because it needs or wants something. Acknowledge the control you have over what you do for others.

This will lead you to consider what qualities you expect and anticipate in their own lives. To what extent does your quality of life involve control over certain aspects of your life? To what extent did you lose control in your relationship with a narcissist? What do you need to get back? How would it improve your quality of life to get it back?

Once you have identified these examples of things you no longer have control of what you would like to regain control over, you can adjust these activities to feel that sense of control. They will give you the feeling of control along with the acceptance of that which you genuinely have no control over, regardless of who you are in a relationship with.

Gardening

Gardening, like pets and walks, inspires questions about nature. Why do certain plants thrive in certain kinds of soil? What determines the color of a flower? Why aren't our tomatoes as big as the tomatoes at the grocery store? Gardening is a way to learn about nature, be humbled by nature, and interact with the environment.

One activity is playing with potting soil. Children must dig in the dirt. Experience sand, wood chips, or whatever the playground provides. It is good to learn the difference between one type of ground and another. You might discover fascinating things about the difference between soil types and why certain plants thrive in a kind of soil, but not another.

Consider that when you were in a relationship with a narcissist, it was like you were planted in the wrong soil. You could not grow there. The environment was not right. You were not getting the proper nutrients. The narcissist was like a weed, taking from you without sharing anything or giving anything back.

A second activity is to look for seeds and consider what kinds of plants grow best in your location. Compare your situation to the importance of specific conditions for certain plants to grow. Acknowledge that no matter how much potential a seed has, it will not grow in certain weather conditions. Your relationship with a narcissist was like being planted in a place with the wrong weather conditions.

A third activity is, of course, planting. Touch the soil. Learn how to plant something. Label what you have planted. Share your plant's progress with others. Be proud of what you have done. Remember that you control everything about your plant that is within your control. You control its placement, soil, water, and anything else you have decided to take. You can't control the weather, but you can control where your plant goes. You will learn how much of your environment is under your control once you plant things.

A fourth activity is measuring growth. It is incredible to watch things evolve. Observe the difference day-to-day and week-to-week. Measure its height. Count leaves. Take notes. Acknowledge your part in its growth. You controlled so much of its potential to become anything more than a seed.

A fifth activity is growing herbs and learning the healing aspect of certain herbs. Marvel at the uses of different herbs. Consider whether everything we need in this world to heal ourselves can be grown if we only utilize the resources at our disposal.

You might even discover some herbs that may help you relax. Relaxation will help with your recovery. You may also find herbs that heal your body, which will also be an aid toward your emotional recovery. The body and the mind are both better when each is well.

The sixth activity is observing roots. Whether you're planting root vegetables like potatoes or pulling weeds, roots are fascinating things to examine.

Think about what root is and consider the importance of roots in the garden and life. Remember that your roots are more important than whatever the narcissist you were with added to your branches.

A seventh activity is cleaning up. Gardening is a messy activity, but the organization is key. Make sure you take on the activity of keeping a clean look to your garden. Your organized lines in the garden will give you a sense of order in life. Think about the correlation between aesthetics and useful boundaries. The narcissist in your life probably understood aesthetics, but not limits. On the other hand, you actively make aesthetically pleasing boundaries in your garden with the knowledge that both are good.

The eighth activity is using gardening tools. Using tools will help you feel in control. Learning to wield a gardening tool is as (or more) useful as wielding any kind of tool one can think of. If you can control the objects in your hands, you can control the thoughts in your mind.

Perhaps gardening and taking care of your pet is not entirely enough for you to be sure you have regained all control you have lost, but it is certainly a start. Think about all the things you do have control over. You haven't lost control. The narcissist you were with only made you think you had. You have it. Activities like caring for a pet and tending to your garden will remind you how much control you still have.

Practice these things often. If these activities don't appeal to you, find something that accomplishes the same tasks. Find another way to use tools. Find another way to see how much of your life is in your hands.

Chapter 29:
Ways to Overcome Codependency

T o overcome codependency and abuse is to love yourself and give yourself a priority. Love comes out of a good feeling, and you enjoy staying in the presence of others without thinking or wanting to change them in any way.

Follow Your Passions

One of the best ways to love yourself is by following your passions. You need to understand that the keys to your happiness are in your hands alone. You will be filled with regret and discontent when you decide to forego your passions or help someone else by not prioritizing your needs. You do not need to cross oceans. A small step every day towards what you love is enough to make you feel happy and content. If you are still unsure about your passion, you can try and think about all those things that stimulate you.

Also, when you choose to follow your passion, your life will be filled with a sense of purpose that you did not have before. And this purpose will be centered on your happiness and not please someone else. Gradually, when you see that your dreams are now becoming a reality, you will gain self-confidence, and your self-esteem will start growing. Set micro-goals towards your goal, and the moment you achieve a micro goal, celebrate that success and give a pat on your back for your victory towards recovery.

Compliment Yourself

Compliments bring enthusiasm and encouragement, but should you depend on someone else for these compliments? The answer is no. You should be your positive support. Appreciate yourself and repeat the compliments repeatedly. Don't take yourself for granted because if you do, others will do the same. Notice that good in yourself, acknowledge them, and compliment them. The moment you hear the encouragement from yourself, you will feel good and energized. But you also must remove every ounce of self-doubt from your body and pay heed to even the smallest achievements you make.

All of this is very much correlated. Positive encouragement leads to positive action. This is because if you hear compliments, you will be motivated to work better and take actions that fetch better results for your well-being. This, in turn, will increase your levels of confidence, and you will continue cheering yourself forward, and the cycle of positivity will go on and on. Wake up every morning and compliment yourself for even the simplest things, and you will never feel alone or need anyone to complete you.

Choose Your Friends Carefully

Your friends have a huge impact on the quality of your life. Your friends can affect not only your mental health but also your physical well-being. If the social circle you stay in always spreads negativity or hurls hurtful words, you should leave them at once. Your mind will constantly be at pain if you are with such a group of people.

If you are surrounded by people who love you from the bottom of their hearts, you will feel good about yourself. They will shower you with their kind words and make you feel positive. Supportive relationships can help codependents break away from their dependency.

Learn to Forgive Yourself for Your Self-Perceived Mistakes

Loving yourself has some barriers that you need to overcome, and one of the most common ones is forgiving yourself for the things that you have done in the past. It can be anything. Sometimes you might be feeling bad about how you treated your ex a couple of years back. Or it can be something that you did in school, which you now think was unfair. If you resonate with this feeling and have such painful memories that keep cropping up in your mind, you need to forgive yourself. Self-forgiveness paves the path to self-love.

You must remind yourself that you did what you could have done at that time. You might not have had the maturity to understand that what you were doing could hurt someone else. But what is important is that you realize it now and you know that you are not going to repeat your mistake. Forgiving yourself might not be easy, and it will entirely depend upon the emotional wound that you have. If the wound is too deep, forgiveness will take time.

Have Enough Sleep

If you want to be happy, you also need to have a well-rested brain, and so you need to sleep properly. Prepare a proper routine and stick to it. Even research has shown that sleep is directly related to the overall happiness of a human being. Your tendency to become depressed increases by many folds whenever you are sleep deprived. This is because when you lack sleep, your stress hormones begin increasing. Sleep deprivation also leads to weight gain and several other health problems. When you are well-rested, you are more patient while talking and communicating with others. This eliminates the chances of misunderstandings.

The moment you sleep well, you can get rid of all these problems and fight anxiety. You will not be fatigued easily and thus complete all your tasks on time. This will make you happy and content.

Work on Self-Trust

The more self-reliant you are, the happier you will be. Do you expect others to do things for you? Do you easily get affected by what other people think of you? Do you always expect people to be there for you? In the case of codependents, most of the answers will be yes. That is how codependents are. But when you start trusting yourself and build your own identity, you do not have to depend on others. When you give up on self-trust, you will become needier, and you will allow toxic people to shatter you and manipulate you. You need to have your voice. Don't shy away from situations of confrontation.

Don't run away from setbacks. Treat them as a learning opportunity because that is what they are. The way you behave in the face of adversity will determine a lot of things about your character. If you lose your courage in times of need, you will grow to hate yourself for it. Your self-image will become lowered in your own eyes, and this will bring discontent. But if you increase your self-trust, you will live without any regrets holding you back.

Be Grateful

How often do you practice gratitude? Are you thankful for the things you have in life? Do you thank the universe every morning because of the necessities of life? If not, you should start doing these things because of one simple reason—they will bring you happiness. When you are grateful, you will be focusing on the good things in life and the good qualities of yourself. You will see that you are not that bad you imagine yourself to be. This will bring about self-love.

Being generous and considering everyone's point of view before responding will make you a better person. This will bring happiness from within, and you will love yourself. This will also help you in dealing with the frustrations of life.

Stop Trying to Be Perfect

Perfectionism kills self-love. No one is perfect, and everyone makes mistakes at some point or the other. Life is not a 'do or die' situation where you must be perfect or fail. There is a middle ground, and that is what life is about. When you try to lead a life free of mistakes, you are always tensed and loathe yourself for the simplest things. You become too hard on yourself, and in this way, you will never be able to enjoy the true essence of life. Sometimes, you end up learning a lot of things when things don't go as planned.

Perfectionism also compels you to compare yourself with others constantly. This brings about a competition that you must live up to the expectations that others have set for you. But if you start leading your life for yourself and not for others, you will realize that everyone is unique, and you are too. So, try to be the best version of yourself and not better than someone else. Give your best in everything that you do, but don't compare your efforts to that of others.

Chapter 30:
Establishing Independence

A person may choose to end a life of codependency for several reasons. When people are trapped in a codependent relationship, they spend their lives serving others' needs and desires. Once that person decides they want to spend their life pursuing their personal goals and ambitions, it becomes necessary to escape any codependent relationships. Only then can the individual be free from the burden of serving others and begin to live a life for themselves, one that enables them to pursue their dreams and find the happiness they deserve.

Define Yourself as an Individual

The first step toward establishing independence is to begin defining yourself as an individual. Anyone who lives their life in codependence will acquire a self-image that is akin to a hive mentality. Rather than being a single person with personal feelings, thoughts, dreams, and goals, they see themselves as part of a collective. Even if that collective comprises only two people, it is still enough to know the individual loses all sense of individuality. Instead, they take on the needs and desires of the taker, who dominates the relationship, thereby defining the nature of all involved. This hive-like mindset can be tough to break, especially for someone who has spent years in a codependent environment. However, it must be broken, but it is replaced with an independent mindset, healthy and strong, and enables the individual to retake control of their life.

When changing from a shared mindset to an individual mindset, list all of your current thoughts, feelings, dreams, and goals on a piece of paper. Most of these thoughts, feelings, dreams, and goals will not necessarily be yours. Once you have created your list, identify each entry as something that belongs to you or something that comes from someone else's heart and mind. How you mark the items on your list is up to you, the important thing is that you differentiate those things that are yours from those things that aren't.

Take the items that made the cut, namely those that belong to you, and create a new list. This new list will start your new life, one that is focused on chasing those dreams that come from your heart and mind, not the heart and mind of another person.

Once you make this distinction, you can clear your heart and mind of the ambitions that came from others, thereby making room for those hopes and desires that are yours alone. This will enable you to focus your energies on those things that will bring happiness and meaning into your life, thus creating the life you deserve.

Discover Your Hopes and Dreams

After you have cleared your mind of the thoughts, hopes, desires, and dreams that weren't yours, you can begin to fill it with those that genuinely belongs to you. However, most people at this stage struggle to come up with a list of any significance, both in terms of length as well as in terms of substance. The few items they can list out usually seem relatively trivial, especially compared to the grandiose schemes that they had been expected to fulfill on behalf of the taker in their codependent relationships. Discovering your hopes and dreams is to sit down and ask yourself one simple question, "If I could do anything with my life, what would I do?"

It may come down to spending time in the outside world to find inspiration and ideas. After all, most victims of codependent relationships live very sheltered and controlled lives. Therefore, they don't always know the available options when it comes to creating an independent life. The important thing is to take all the time you need to find what inspires you. Once you find inspiration, be sure to write it down to start pursuing that goal and finding the happiness that you deserve.

Breaking free from the influences of codependency can take a lot more time and effort than most people realize. Therefore, always be sure to take all the time and effort you need to achieve real and lasting freedom. Only then you can live a life that brings you pure joy and meaning.

Determine Your Direction

Now that you have compiled a list of your hopes and dreams, you can begin to take the next step to determine your direction. Depending on your dreams and goals, you might only need to consider getting a better job or a better place to live. Create a goal that will bring the most happiness and meaning into your life. Develop a clear list of all your hopes and dreams. This list will present specific patterns, and it is those patterns that will determine the direction you need to take to achieve the life of your dreams. For some people, the list will consist largely of things oriented around a job or career. Whether it's about making more money, finding a more challenging job, or pursuing the career of your dreams, in this case, your direction will be job oriented.

Alternatively, your list might consist of items of a different nature, such as making friends, finding a person to share your life with, or even starting a family. If the pattern of your list is more about love and friendship than of money and career, then you need to steer your life in the appropriate direction. Rather than spending all your time fixated on your job or your finances, you need to spend your time and efforts socializing. Start spending time with any friends you currently have, especially in such settings like parties or social gatherings where you can meet new people. By exposing yourself to more people, you can start to make new friends or even start looking to engage in relationships of a more intimate nature. The key is to break out of the bubble you lived in as a victim of codependency and expand your social and romantic horizons. If love and friendship are where you will find happiness, you need to make those your new priorities.

Create a Plan

Once you have determined the direction your life needs to take to become a happy and fulfilling life, you both desire and deserve, the final step to achieving independence is to create a plan. While determining a direction and creating a plan may seem to be the same at first, they are two distinctly different processes. Determining direction allows you to come up with the overall goal that will bring happiness into your life. This is a general idea as it was. In contrast, creating a plan is the process of laying out a step-by-step approach that will enable you to achieve your goal.

A good analogy of this is the planning of a vacation. When you plan a vacation, the first thing you do is decide the type of vacation you want. You might want to spend a week hiking in the woods, skiing in the mountains, or just lounging around on a beach. Deciding the type of vacation you want, is the same thing as determining the direction in your life. The next step is to choose a specific destination and plan on how you will get there. You might need to book a flight if your destination is a long way off. If your destination is closer to home, you might only need to choose the route you will drive to get to where you want. This is the process of creating a plan.

The important thing is to focus all your time and energy on achieving your goal, taking each of the necessary steps carefully and thoughtfully, thereby giving yourself the best chance of success. Researching the best methods for creating resumes or taking interviews, for example, might be another step you take to increase your chances of success.

This goes back to the concept of knowing when to ask for help. If you feel overwhelmed when trying to create the plan that will take you to the life of your dreams, rather than simply giving up or putting forth a half-hearted attempt, find someone who can help you to create the plan that will enable you to achieve your goal. Remember that you deserve the life of your dreams, and you are worth every effort required to turn those dreams into reality.

Chapter 31:
Building Self-Esteem

I f you had confidence before your relationship, the narcissist has likely taken that away from you. The most daunting task in your recovery process is to build a new sense of confidence, different than you had before. This can only come as you make your self-esteem and your perception of who you are and who you want to be. So, maybe you didn't have a bunch of confidence back then either, which is why it is crucial to start building it now so that you can feel what you do deserve—worthy and appreciated from yourself.

The good news is that by following the last two suggestions, forgiving yourself, and learning to listen to your intuition, you will also be building self-awareness, which promotes confidence. Through these three steps, your goals bring your awareness levels to a place where you can look at how the narcissist hurt you and which areas you need to work on the most. Which will tell you your strengths and weaknesses, and in the process of working through your weaknesses, with everyone you overcome, your confidence level will go up as well.

Building confidence cannot be done unless you investigate the traumatic experiences you endured even before the narcissistic relationship. It could stem from childhood, learn to break down, and walk through these barriers to help you see just how strong you really are, which will build a new level of confidence. Reaching out to support systems and teams like groups, classes, therapies, family, and friends, you will learn how to develop self-reflection. Self-reflection is crucial in learning more about yourself, and how you can see all the beautiful qualities the narcissist made you blind to. Take the pain that you feel, and use it to learn more about yourself, and you may find out new things you have never seen about yourself before. By lighting up this whole new perception of yourself, you will find success and inner peace, which often leads to happiness.

Learning how to trust again is no easy task, but with patience and self-kindness, and the help of others, it is possible. When you have successfully learned how to reach inside yourself and trust who matters, then you can start putting your trust in new people who come into your life. This is because with the trust you feel inside yourself, you can trust that you know best when you are going to put your faith in someone else. This happens when you are perfectly in tune with your intuition. When you are in tune with your intuition, you will only follow your gut instinct if you have the confidence to believe that you are right. And with forgiveness of your mistakes, you make along the way and patience to overcome whatever problems lie ahead for you, and you will finally learn the true meaning of trust in yourself and others.

When someone has low self-esteem, they are more vulnerable to narcissists and other people and situations that are mostly negative. Narcissists look for those with low self-esteem because they know that it will make it easier to get them into their web. When you have good self-esteem, you have a healthy level of self-respect and confidence in your abilities and worth. When self-esteem is low, someone is more likely to tolerate abusive situations, not live up to their potential, and become depressed.

Self-esteem is a part of everything that you do in life. It affects your performance at school, work, and in your relationships. Low self-esteem can also stop you from living a full life since it is characterized by the fear of trying new things or test your limits.

Self-esteem ultimately comes from within. However, some factors can influence it. The people around you play a role in how you see yourself. This is especially true when it comes to those close to you and those you respect. For example, if a parent is always critical of a child, this can damage the child's self-esteem. On the other hand, when a parent is very supportive, it helps someone see their value, leading to healthy self-esteem.

Every person has that inner voice that essentially tells them what to think of themselves. For some, this inner voice can be highly negative and critical. When this happens, it is easy to believe the voice and feel as though you are inferior. It is common to have negative feelings, but when you allow them to dominate you, you eventually start believing them. It is important to listen to negative feelings, but then put them into perspective. If your inner voice tells you that you are a failure and listen to it and do not question it, you will start to believe this, resulting in lower self-esteem.

Comparing yourself to other people is another influencer on your self-esteem. It is fine to evaluate those around you, but do not allow this to overshadow your strengths. Taking inventory of your weaknesses and strengths and focusing on what you are good can help prevent the strengths of those around you from negatively impacting how you view yourself.

Improving Your Self-Esteem

The good news is that if you have low self-esteem, this does not have to remain. There are ways to boost and alleviate the negative thoughts and feelings from dominating your view of yourself. To get started, work on developing life skills that contribute to how you see yourself and the world around you. These include:

- Do not be afraid to identify and experience your feelings. When you push feelings down and try to ignore them, they will eventually come to the surface.

- Do not be afraid to detach yourself from negative situations and people.

- Be receptive to those around you and empathize with people.

- Think optionally and not in black and white. This allows you to solve problems better and learn new things.

- Be assertive when it is needed. Do not allow others to dictate the direction of your life.

Focus on the good things in your life and what you are good at. Low self-esteem can make it seem like you are not good enough at anything. However, when you reflect on the good, it is easier to remember that it exists on days when you are feeling down.

Make a learning opportunity out of every mistake. Every person fails and makes mistakes. This is a part of life. However, please do not dwell on these and the negative consequences that might come with them. Spend an hour being upset because it is important to experience your emotions. However, after an hour, go into action mode and consider why the mistake or failure occurred. You will always be able to find at least one lesson. This lesson reduces the risk of mistakes and failure in the future.

Know that perfection is not possible. What is important is that you are putting in the effort and working on learning and getting better. No person is born being great at everything. Life is all about learning and working on developing the skills needed to achieve your goals.

Remember that every person has their strengths. Imagine a world where every person is just good at everything. There would be no healthy competition, no learning, and no balance. Know your strengths and respect the strengths of others.

Know what you cannot change. For example, if you are short, you are short. You cannot change this. Once you accept what cannot be changed, you can start putting your focus on your life areas that can be improved.

Do not be afraid to try. You never know what you are good at until you test your limits. Have you always wanted to play soccer, but were afraid you were not good enough? Get a game going with friends or join a local team. You may be great, or you may not. Either way, you tried it, and every new thing you try expands your horizons.

Give yourself credit when you deserve it. When you do something great, be proud of yourself. It is easy to put more focus on flaws because this is just what humans do. However, when you switch your focus to the good stuff, your self-esteem will get a boost.

Chapter 32:
Indications That You Are Recovering from Narcissistic Trauma and Abuse

With everything that we have learned so far, whether you have started your recovery from the abuse, you may be wondering if you have even taken steps forward. Sometimes, it can feel as though you have taken steps forward, but many steps back. With this frame of mind, you may feel motivated to strive for success, and less inspired if you don't feel any different than when you started. The truth is, with every step forward, practicing the many techniques and strategies, you will be on the right path, even when it doesn't feel like it. You may question whether you have made any progress because you still may be thinking or wondering about your abuser. You may miss the moments you shared due to the cognitive dissonances the narcissist has implemented. This will cloud your vision and taking any more steps forward may feel like an impossible task.

Pay attention to the following signs, as these signs are clear indications that you are recovering.

1. **You realize and understand that self-care is an everyday priority** – This first

sign is that you have finally come to the acceptance that you are taking steps forward when you put yourself first. Self-care is perhaps the utmost importance in recovering from your past trauma and abuse. Self-care may include saying no more often, taking a nap when you feel overwhelmed or tired, eating healthier, exercising daily, creating boundaries, and making wiser decisions. You are so focused on putting yourself first, that you don't feel like you have time for "drama."

2. **You do everything you have to, to protect your physical and mental well-being** – You notice the identity of a narcissist, and you realize that their feelings were never real. You understand the pain you went through, or are going through currently, and have vowed not to let it happen again. You do not allow yourself to respond to their hoovering techniques and understand that things will get better if you continue down this path. You have come to terms with the fact that you will no longer tolerate or accept being around negative influences and going back into a narcissistic relationship. You have a new sense of peace and have set boundaries to continue feeling happier than you were.

3. **You don't care about what your ex thinks** – Remember the time where you were sitting there, after your separation, and you wondered if they were thinking about you, what they were doing, and how they were living their lives without you. Maybe you missed them and wondered if they missed you too. You are now in a place where you don't think about or wonder those things because you are fulfilling your dreams, desires, ambitions, etc. You no longer spend time thinking about their hold over you, or what they think, because you don't have the time or patience to.

4. **You are more focused on your own life than what your ex is doing with theirs** – Because you know that if you go back to your ex, you will only be living with the repeated abuse that you experienced before, you no longer care to be engaged with them. You are at a state where you have worked hard to get where you are now and realize that the most important thing is to take care of yourself.

5. **You come up with solutions, rather than focus on your problems** – You have realized that you have the power and strength to change your circumstances. You have accepted that control, and power is in your

hands, and not theirs. There is a reaction for every action, and it's your choice how you decide to respond. If you get an email from your abuser, instead of having the urge to read it, you delete it. When you get a text, you find it easy to ignore it. When you see them or run into them, there are no longer the "in love" feelings you once had.

6. **You see the past abuse as an opportunity rather than a punishment like you once had** – Regardless of your low self-esteem or unconfident behaviors were stemmed from your childhood or not, you now realize that going through the relationship of a narcissist was an opportunity to overcome these weaknesses. You no longer look at your ex, or anyone else for approval, or appreciation. You have come to a state of mind where you are strong enough to walk away from anyone who makes you believe against your beliefs and devalue who you are. You have officially become your own best friend instead of your worst enemy, and you are now clear about why you experienced the abuse and forgive yourself because where you are now is where you need to be.

Chapter 33:
Getting Rid of Codependent Communication

I f you were to record a fight between yourself and your significant other, you may just realize that codependency has reared its ugly head during the argument. You must create a vocabulary and some communication skills that will move you out of codependency to interdependency. This is like learning how to speak any new language.

You must take responsibility for how you communicate. You must build a bridge that leads away from your true self while pursuing genuine connections with other people.

You Need to Focus on "I"

A critical part of learning to communicate well is learning how to use "I" messages. This tool is used when training Unites States diplomats. It was created about 50 years ago by our government. You can find this message outlined on the United States Department of State's website. Now, the "I" message is a skill that is also taught during the couple's therapy. You will learn how to use this tool, too.

Shifting Internally

When you use an "I" message, it will restructure how you think, and it will make you self-reflect before you speak. Since language shapes our reality, every time you use "I" instead of "YOU" when you try to resolve conflicts, you change your internal reality. This will force you to identify and process how you feel and how you perceive things before your mouth opens to speak about the problem.

The "I" Formula

The "I" message has three components: how you are feeling, what has caused you to feel like this, and the reasons behind why you have these feelings. It will look something like this: "I feel (a feeling, not thoughts) when you (a nonjudgmental description of behavior) because (a reason why you are feeling how you feel)." If you were to fill in the blanks, it might look a bit like this: "I feel threatened when you scream at me to turn off the radio because music helps me relax."

The wonderful part of excellent communication is each person values and respects the other's opinion, and it doesn't matter just how different they are. They will accept the other person's right to think and feel the way they do, and this begins the start of a wonderful compromise.

Example:

Jacob hates it when Rhianna leaves her beauty products all over the bathroom vanity. He has asked her numerous times to put all her stuff away when she gets through with it. Every time Rhianna tries to explain why she didn't, she forgot, she was in a hurry, she can leave faster if she doesn't take time to put it up, or there isn't room for all her stuff to be put away. She keeps promising every time that she will start being more aware, but each day the products remain on the vanity.

Every time Jacob finds her stuff on the counter, he gets madder and madder inside. He gives up on trying changing Rhianna, but each time they argue about something, he will always bring up how inconsiderate she is when she leaves her products on the bathroom counter because she knows it bothers him.

The big question is, who owns the problem? Some people might say that it is Rhianna's because she won't put her things away. If Jacob didn't care that she left her things on the counter, they wouldn't have a problem, would they?

Own Your Feelings

Learning how to communicate in ways that will encourage people to take responsibility for their feelings is one way to begin resolving conflicts. If you were to look at Jacob and Rhianna's therapy session, it starts with Jacob saying he has a problem.

Conflicts happen when you are in a relationship, so learning ways to move through them always and smoothly will enforce new behaviors. Every couple needs to be invested in communicating well with each other because there will be immediate payoffs.

Power Struggle

Many couples make the mistake of getting in a battle with one another when problems come up. Each contestant steps on a platform where they will try to defend their truth. From their positions, every opponent will try every weapon they have in their arsenal to defeat their enemy and knock them off their platform while remaining steadfast in their truth. The person who is left standing will be right and will be the winner of the battle.

Weapons That Are Used to Be Right

- "This is crazy, silly, mean, or ridiculous. You are upset about that?" This weapon is called the "what is the matter with you." You turn their concern back at them and while discounting all possibilities that their opponent could have real problems because they are flawed. This causes them to be wrong.

- "That isn't what I felt, did, or said, and that isn't what you said or did." This weapon is called rewriting history. It is used to prove what their opponent remembers is false. They won't know what truly happened, and they will always be wrong.

- "How can you say that?" This gets accompanied by tears or anger. This weapon is called the "shut up. I can't handle this." You attack your opponent for some negative fault or for being insensitive. You emphasize they are wrong for trying to resolve the problem. Their main goal is to make them feel bad, so they go away.

- "This is unfair. I would never get upset about something like this." This weapon is called the "shame on you or the self-righteous." It is meant to stop their opponent by saying they are crazy for having any concerns. They are wrong for even feeling how you feel.

- "That pisses me off." This is called the "shut up, or I will show you what anger truly is" weapon. It gets used to a person's opponent's concerns back on them. It will deflate and divert their concerns by blaming them, and these discounts their rights to have concerns. This means they are wrong.

Affirmation

This skill sets a tone for compromise and resolution. If your significant other states a concern, the first thing you must do is affirm. Most people will get defensive automatically. You must affirm in a way that is nondefensively that you heard their concerns. You can do this by repeating what your significant other has said in your own words. Partner: "Why haven't you finished the laundry?" You: "You thought I would have the laundry done by now?" From this point, the tone has been established. "I have heard from you, now let's talk about it." You have let the wind out of their angry sails and show you are a person who will listen to their concerns and move on.

Affirmation isn't what you use at the beginning of the discussion. You use it all the way to get information from your partner and let them know you are there and want to help fix the problem. Here is an example:

Partner: "You were home all day. Why didn't you get all the flowers planted?"

You: "You wanted it finished today before it started raining tomorrow."

The first time you use this skill with your significant other, they might look at you like you've gone crazy. Many people will just wait for you to get defensive before they even get to say their complaints. Most of the time, they are already planning what they are going to say after getting angry and defensive.

Validation

Affirmation and validation are interchangeable. Each one can create a spirit of cooperation, and many times they are used together. Validation could be used to accept how your partner feels. If you add validation after affirmation, it could sound something like:

You: "You thought I would have the flowers planted by now. I can understand why you would feel this way. It is dark now, and it's supposed to rain tomorrow."

Even though this is important, if couples could learn to communicate, especially if there is a conflict, they don't use much validation or affirmation.

You need to be aware of how well you are listening. Do you listen totally without beginning to get defensive in your head? Being internal is the first thing to do. You must completely focus on what your partner is saying rather than figure out your comeback. If you can't understand what they are saying, get clarification before you get defensive.

Affirmation and validation are going to take practice. Focus on what your partner is saying, totally listen, and acknowledge you have heard them by affirming what they said. "You think I should finish the dishes now." Ask some questions if you must clarify what you heard. "What is bothering you? Is it the dishes sitting in the sink?" Don't ever rush a response. Validate. You don't have to agree with your significant other. You just must validate they have the right to feel what they are feeling. "It doesn't matter if they sit there until after we have walked the dog. I understand that clutter bothers you, and you seem frustrated. Is this it?"

These simple but effective skills pack some power. When therapists introduce these two couples, they might try to discount them initially, resist following through, or even feel awkward.

When talking about codependent relationships, there will be many things happening underneath the level of communication. It will be hard for some people to admit they don't know how to talk to their significant other.

It might be very uncomfortable for a person who is codependent to show their weakness during therapy. It might be hard for them to ask for what they want.

Conclusion

U nderstanding the dynamics of codependent relationships and how narcissists try to keep them alive should awaken you to what you probably must do next is to end the relationship. You are undoubtedly a victim and see how your patterns and personality traits contributed to the cycle of codependency. The narcissist is the one who caused you to feel worthless and weak, so they are to blame for what you went through—not you. However, the only way out of this toxic relationship is to halt your participation in it.

The next time you and your partner go through a rough patch, don't teach them that you are swayed by their recapture strategies. Teach them that you have no response to them at all.

One of the most useful tips is that narcissists can't stand indifference. They can feed off positive and negative attention alike, but if you pay them no mind at all, they will learn that they can't source narcissistic supply from you and move on.

This is especially important to remember when you do "no contact." They will try to contact you in every way possible, but if you act like you don't care, either way, the narcissist will realize you aren't useful to them anymore.

After you decisively put an end to the relationship, many thoughts will fly through your head. They will include thoughts of doubt and relief. Now that you can think about what your ex put you through more clearly, you will have space to focus on yourself. Once you are ready to date again, you will be able to spot a narcissist from a mile away. When that happens, run like hell.

Most importantly, you know that with a healthy sense of identity and self-worth, you can't be manipulated by narcissistic people. The narcissist saw you as insecure and used it to their advantage.

You won't be vulnerable to a narcissist's charms ever again because now, you know the forms they take. You also won't care about flattery because you will already know yourself. You won't need someone else to tell you if you are smart, beautiful, or anything else. You already know these things.

Sometimes, pain is necessary to feel. None of the pain that you went through when the narcissist put you down was necessary to feel, but the pain you feel from letting them go is necessary. They put you through a lot when you were together, and unfortunately, it is a fact that you will have to go through some more pain when you break up with them.

Like you will learn how to let them go, you will learn how to let go of what they think of you. Because of "no contact," you won't hear what they think of you, either. All the echoes of what they used to say will exist in your head and your head alone. Over time, these echoes naturally fade.

The less you care about what your ex thinks of you, the further you are in recovering yourself.

You already know yourself. Since the narcissist took so much out of you, you just weren't the center of your attention for a very long time. You can move on from that stage in your life now. When you realize how wonderful it is to be free of their demands, you will exhale deeply. It feels like you are a new person. But you aren't a new person—you just remembered about yourself again.

Your friends and family will be relieved that you aren't together, too. If you didn't tell them the truth about the relationship before, you could feel free to tell them about it now. They will understand why you weren't open to them. You will be surprised by how many people have had experiences with narcissists. They are like the flu that everyone has had. Once they are over it, they sure are glad it is over. You are running out of excuses to stay in this toxic situation if you still are.

You know now, and it's time to put it into action.

The longer you allow yourself to stay in this situation, the harder it will be to get out of it. Everything that was in your life before this relationship will seem farther and farther away until the narcissist is the thing you know most. You don't want to reach this point.

The longer you spend around a person, the more of an effect they have on you. This means narcissists' spell becomes stronger the longer it takes for you to leave them. If you think it is hard for you to leave now, it will be even harder if you wait another month.

It will be hard to make this change, no matter how much time you give yourself. It will be hard today; it will be hard next week; it would have been hard last week. Timing isn't important. No matter when you do it, you must resist everything your codependency tells you to do and cut them off.

Abuse is never the fault of the victim, but sadly, we all must defend ourselves in this world. An unwavering idea of who you are will protect you from all forms of psychological abuse. Some people use mental and emotional tricks to exploit you, but if your mind's "self-concept" room has sturdy walls, narcissists will have no luck trying to tear them down.

Printed in Great Britain
by Amazon